General Editor: Robin Gilmour

Contemporary Women Novelists

FLORA ALEXANDER

Lecturer in English, University of Aberdeen

Edward Arnold
A division of Hodder & Stoughton
LONDON NEW YORK MELBOURNE AUCKLAND

© 1989 Flora Alexander

First published in Great Britain 1989

Distributed in the USA by Routledge, Chapman and Hall, Inc.
29 West 35th Street, New York, NY 10001

British Library Cataloguing in Publication Data

Alexander, Flora
    Contemporary women novelists. — (Modern fiction)
    1. Fiction in English. Women writers, 1945 —
    Critical studies
    I. Title II. Series
    823'.914'099287

    ISBN 0-7131-6557-X

Typeset in 10/12 pt Sabon Compugraphic
by Colset Private Limited, Singapore
Printed and bound in Great Britain for Edward Arnold, the
educational, academic and medical publishing division of Hodder
and Stoughton Limited, 41 Bedford Square, London WC1B 3DQ
by Biddles Ltd, Guildford and King's Lynn

Contents

General Editor's Preface

Fiction constitutes the largest single category of books published each year, and the discussion of fiction is at the heart of the present revolution in literary theory, yet the reader looking for substantial guidance to some of the most interesting prose writers of the twentieth century – especially those who have written in the past 30 or 40 years – is often poorly served. Specialist studies abound, but up-to-date maps of the field are harder to come by. *Modern Fiction* has been designed to supply that lack. It is a new series of authoritative introductory studies of the chief writers and movements in the history of twentieth-century fiction in English. Each volume has been written by an expert in the field and offers a fresh and accessible reading of the writer's work in the light of the best recent scholarship and criticism. Biographical information is provided, consideration of the writer's relationship to the world of their times, and detailed readings of selected texts. The series includes short-story writers as well as novelists, contemporaries as well as the classic moderns and their successors, Commonwealth writers as well as British and American; and there are volumes on themes and groups as well as on individual figures. At a time when twentieth-century fiction is increasingly studied and talked about, *Modern Fiction* provides short, helpful, stimulating introductions designed to encourage fresh thought and further enquiry.

Robin Gilmour

In grateful memory of
my mother, Emily Jane Hill and
my father, Angus William Ross

Preface

Although women have been writing novels for more than two centuries now, they are probably more active as writers of fiction today than they have ever been before. During the last 20 years there have been vigorous developments in thinking about women and about their roles in society, and important changes have followed upon these new ideas. The novelists considered in this book have had writing careers that largely coincide with this period of intensive argument about women. Not all are feminists, but even those who are indifferent to feminism, or critical of it, like Alice Thomas Ellis, are living and writing in a world in which feminism is a force that cannot be avoided. For some of them, for instance Angela Carter and Sara Maitland, it has been a major influence and source of material. Between them these novelists produce a wide spectrum of fictional responses to a changing world. I have chosen to write about a generation who began writing in England in the 60s and 70s, and to see them in relation to some of the changes that have taken place in the last 20 years. Three of the most outstanding women writing today in the tradition of the English novel, Iris Murdoch, Muriel Spark, and Doris Lessing, are not discussed here, because they belong to an older generation, and they have already been well served by critics. I wish to focus attention on writers who are younger and have received less critical consideration. Murdoch, Spark and Lessing, all happily still active, are to be seen as important predecessors of the women who are the subject of this study.

The propriety of writing about women novelists as a group is sometimes questioned, not least by women writers themselves, who may sense that there is something condescending about a critical approach which selects them and implies that they are different from men. This is part of a larger division of opinion between those women who refuse to entertain the idea that their intellectual and imaginative lives are in any significant way different from the lives of men, and others who argue that women's lives are indeed different from men's lives, but that their experience is no less important and interesting. A.S. Byatt, for example, has said that the writer's profession is one of the few where immense sexual-political battles do not have to be fought, and that for her, literature has been a way of escape from the limits of being female. I make the assumption that being female is significantly different from being male, even for women who are childless, and who do little or no domestic work, because of the inescapable fact that in our culture a person perceived to be female is treated differently from a male person, both in individual relationships and by society in general. For all the novelists I deal with, the fact of their gender has had some effect on their experience and their perceptions of the world, and this is in some measure reflected in the nature of the fiction they write. To privilege gender, as I do here, is to focus on certain aspects of their work (although by no means on a narrow range of topics) in full awareness that there are many more things which could be said about them in differently angled studies. I hope it is not really necessary to say that writing about them as women novelists does not imply that they are less than 'proper' novelists, any more than writing about Irish poets would imply that an Irish poet is not a true poet.

Although something is inevitably lost if English fiction is considered separately from the work of, for example, Toni Morrison, Marge Piercy and Margaret Atwood, there is also something to be gained by concentrating on a group of writers who have in common the cultural background of British experience. The ten novelists I have chosen to write about present responses to, if not the same world, then worlds that are closely linked. They present a rich variety of material in equally varied forms. Any classification of their work must be tentative, and I have arranged them in three groups on a very simple basis. In Chapter 2 I deal with Margaret Drabble, Anita Brookner and A.S. Byatt, who although they have very different approaches to the writing of fiction are connected by their shared interest in expanding the possibilities of realism. Chapter 3 is devoted to novelists who have a more political stance. Fay Weldon, Zoe Fairbairns, and Pat Barker are not the only feminists in this book, but for them, more than for others, the personal is always and very obviously the political. The novelists treated in Chapter 4, Angela Carter, Emma Tennant, Sara Maitland and Alice Thomas Ellis, have in common that they are all interested in going beyond realism, and make use, in varying proportions, of myth, symbol, metaphor, or fantasy. My first chapter places the literature in the context of contemporary feminism. Readers who do not wish to linger over this material will find that the discussion of the novels begins in Chapter 2.

In the preparation of this book I have incurred a number of debts. I wish to thank Robin Gilmour for the idea out of which the book grew, and for sound advice given generously as it progressed. A term of study leave from the University of Aberdeen enabled me to carry out basic work, and the staff of the Queen Mother Library in Aberdeen have been unfailingly helpful. Conversations with Su Reid have been invaluable in helping me to clarify ideas, and I am also glad to acknowledge a debt to Ruth Edwards and Elizabeth Roberts for useful discussion and information. I am deeply grateful to my husband, who encouraged me to stop reading and start writing, and to Ruth, Jane, Mark and Patrick, who gave me their support, and took an interest in what I was doing.

Note on Editions

Quotations are taken from the following editions:

Pat Barker, *Union Street*, Virago, 1982;
Anita Brookner, *Providence*, Triad Grafton, 1983,
   Hotel du Lac, Triad Grafton, 1985;
A.S. Byatt, *Still Life*, Penguin, 1986;
Angela Carter, *The Magic Toyshop*, Virago, 1981,
   The Sadeian Woman, Virago, 1979,
   Nights at the Circus, Picador, 1985,
   Wayward Girls and Wicked Women (ed.) Virago, 1986;
Margaret Drabble, *The Millstone*, Penguin, 1968,
   The Waterfall, Penguin, 1971,
   The Middle Ground, Penguin, 1981;
Alice Thomas Ellis, *The Sin Eater*, Penguin, 1986,
   The Birds of the Air, Penguin, 1983,
   The 27th Kingdom, Penguin, 1982;
Zoe Fairbairns, *Benefits*, Virago, 1979;
Sara Maitland, *Virgin Territory*, Pavanne, 1985;
Emma Tennant, *The Bad Sister*, Picador, 1979,
   Queen of Stones, Picador, 1983;
Fay Weldon, *Down Among the Women*, Penguin, 1973,
   Praxis, Coronet, 1980,
   Puffball, Coronet, 1981,
   Leader of the Band, Hodder & Stoughton, 1988.

1

Introduction

The Background to Contemporary Feminism

Novelists whose careers have developed since the mid-1960s have been writing in a cultural climate that is deeply affected by contemporary feminism. But the contemporary women's movement possesses a long history. At least some of the political thinkers of the eighteenth century recognized that the rights of man also implied rights for woman. Mary Wollstonecraft's *A Vindication of the Rights of Woman* (1792) is an early milestone on a long journey not yet accomplished. Throughout the nineteenth century arguments continued about the proper sphere of women, and during this time women obtained some limited legal and financial rights, and began to have access to certain professions. The aim of universal suffrage was achieved in Britain in 1928, and in the twentieth century women have generally expected to have more independence and wider opportunities. The two world wars had a significant effect on perceptions of what women were capable of doing. In each war women were encouraged to undertake work in the national interest, and child-care facilities were introduced to enable them to do so. The fact of their ability to do 'men's' work could no longer be denied. Yet the return of peace in each case was held to be the signal for a return to 'normality', and women were urged to return to the home to make room for men in the work-place. After the Second World War, in both Britain and America the prevailing social and political thinking was that families should be maintained by male breadwinners, and that women should accept the role of home-makers, which carried with it economic dependence on men. It was not until the 1960s that equal rights and opportunities for women became once more a matter of widespread and lively concern.

The 70s and 80s have been distinguished by what has come to be known as the 'second wave' of feminism. Feminism has become a highly important issue in contemporary thought, and male-devised orthodoxies about women's nature, capacities and roles have been challenged. In the United States Betty Friedan's *The Feminine Mystique* (1963) placed the argument about women firmly on the agenda, and new developments followed quickly thereafter. In the United Kingdom, and also more widely, the appearance in 1962 of Doris Lessing's novel *The Golden Notebook* raised very basic issues about the ways in which women live their lives, and the sort of freedoms they can expect to have. Although Lessing has maintained that she did not see herself as writing a feminist book, the fact remains that the discussion it contains about freedom and autonomy spoke to an audience which was receptive to such ideas and immediately applied them to its own situation. The general radical climate of the 60s nourished the women's movement, although sometimes in an indirect way. Women working alongside men in the struggle for civil rights for black Americans, and in the opposition to the Vietnam war, were frequently bitterly disillusioned by the realization that the democratic instincts of their male colleagues did not extend to accepting the case for women's equal rights. The discovery of this male blindness to reason and justice contributed something to the energy that generated the women's movement at the end of the 60s.

Contemporary Feminism: The Woman's View of the World

Although feminists differ in their analyses of women's oppression, liberal feminists, socialist feminists, and radical feminists share many key concepts. Essentially women argue that in the past the world has been explained almost entirely by men, and that the explanations that resulted have not taken account of the differences that exist between men's perspectives and those of the other half of the human race. Male subjectivity has been mistaken for objectivity. Knowledge about women has been largely produced by men, sometimes with laughable results. Virginia Woolf in *A Room of One's Own* notes the prolific output by men of books about women – books written not only by doctors and biologists, but by 'agreeable essayists, light-fingered novelists, young men who have taken the M.A. degree; men who have taken no degree; men who have no apparent qualification save that they are not women'.[1] She declares England to be 'under the rule of a patriarchy', and this notion of patriarchy – the law of the fathers – is much used today to express the perception that the world has been analysed and controlled by men. Feminists have been challenging patriarchal assumptions, and the result has been a large-scale reconceptualizing of the world to take account of the experience of women.

Traditional ideas about women were based on the view that for one reason or another women were not fit to share power with men. In societies in which power depended on the ability to use physical force, there were reasons for assigning women to different roles. In modern societies in which intellect counts for more than physical strength, and fertility can be controlled, biological differences might be expected to have less importance. Yet patriarchal attitudes have continued to pervade thinking in many areas, so that the concepts that are constructed about the female typically characterize women as lacking, or unacceptable. Alternatively, and just as damagingly, they are seen as 'special' in a way that makes it in male judgement unsuitable for them to have access to power, or to perform roles other than those which are domestic or which involve providing some kind of care or service.

Women's challenging of long-standing assumptions can be seen, for example, in theology, in which feminist scholarship has produced critical re-readings of the Bible, and uncovered lost meanings and traditions. Women have also suggested, sometimes in the face of irrational hostility, that the male language and imagery used in worship should be supplemented by female terminology. In the United States, some of the writing that comes out of the interaction between theology and feminism, notably that of Mary Daly, has been truly revolutionary.[2] Daly vigorously exposes what she sees as the misogyny that lies at the core of the Judaeo-Christian tradition, and in her later work concludes that it is not possible to reform patriarchal society, and argues instead for a separate women's culture. Feminist theology in Britain is more moderate. Sara Maitland, who is discussed in Chapter 4, and who as well as being a writer of fiction has an active interest in theology, confronts the problems of misogyny and patriarchal inflexibility in the church with wit and vigour, and the tensions inherent in this material

1. Virginia Woolf, *A Room of One's Own* (Triad Grafton, 1977), ch 2, pp. 27–8.
2. See Mary Daly, *Beyond God the Father* (The Women's Press, 1986), *Gyn/Ecology: the Metaethics of Radical Feminism* (The Women's Press, 1979), and *Pure Lust: Elemental Feminist Philosophy* (The Women's Press, 1984).

have provided her with a fruitful subject in her novel, *Virgin Territory* (1984). Alice Thomas Ellis, the other Christian novelist discussed here, is by contrast conservative in her religious position. Like Muriel Spark she is a convert to Roman Catholicism, and her novels express a strong attachment to the traditional nature of the church.

Psychology has been one of the major areas of feminist enquiry. Freud has been of particular importance in giving currency to ideas about female psychological development that explain it in terms of lack and negativity, or of not conforming to a norm derived from males. Feminists have subjected to vigorous questioning Freud's attempts to find a female equivalent for the Oedipus complex, his ideas about the existence and implications of penis envy, and his belief that a relatively passive disposition is psychologically normal in the female. They frequently see orthodox Freudian theory as conservative and determinist, and incompatible with their desire for change. Feminist revisions of psychoanalytic theory propose alternative explanations of development of identity. Nancy Chodorow, for example, who has exerted significant influence on feminist thinking, proposes that the mother–infant bond is different in the cases of female and male children, and that this accounts for crucial differences in feminine and masculine personality. The girl comes to define and experience herself as continuous with others, and to have a sense of self which is flexible, whereas the boy defines himself as more separate and distinct. Chodorow's work has provided a useful basis for some feminist theorists working on literature and attempting to identify the specific qualities of women as writers and as readers.[3]

However much they may disagree with him, Freud's work is of compelling interest to contemporary women because it has been central to many modern assumptions about femininity and female desire. Emma Tennant, whose work is considered in Chapter 4, makes playful use of his *Fragment of an Analysis of a Case of Hysteria*, the famous case history of Dora, in her novel *Queen of Stones*, a fiction about adolescent girls. She demonstrates how they are subjected to expectations shaped by fairy-stories and by psychoanalytically based ideas. The male psychological explanations are presented conspicuously within the narrative, and treated subversively. In her presentation of men pronouncing inappropriately on women, and what she describes as a woman using a man's language, Tennant is drawing

---

3. Nancy Chodorow, *The Reproduction of Mothering. Psychoanalysis and the Sociology of Gender* (Berkeley and Los Angeles, University of California Press, 1978), p. 169.

attention to an example of what has been called by Angela Carter a 'colonialization of the mind': a general acceptance of established positions that do not give proper weight to the experience of women. In many other areas, women have objected to approaches that assume without evidence that women's experience is the same as men's, or that see the male as the norm and the female as exceptional. New work in virtually all disciplines introduces a female dimension, or requests that in some way the experience of women should be taken into account.

Contemporary Feminism and Female Experience

The women's movement has scrutinized ideas about female sexuality, and has disputed the traditional thinking that linked women's sexual activity inextricably with the bearing and also the care of children, arguing for their right to be sexually active without committing themselves to responsibility for child-rearing. The importance for women of having control of their own fertility emerges as an issue for many novelists: it is particularly prominent in the work of Pat Barker and Zoe Fairbairns, as is shown in Chapter 3. The idea that women's role in society must be determined by their biological capacity for reproduction has until recently been an important factor in restricting their opportunities. Feminists have looked critically at the assumption that the biological differences between men and women justify the traditional assignment of roles between the sexes. They point to more recent psychological work which shows that, although there are differences between men and women, there are also many similarities, and which questions why it has been customary to emphasize the differences rather than the similarities.[4] Thinking about child-care has been reassessed. The finding of the child psychologist John Bowlby that children require continuity of care, was in the 1950s applied in such an extreme way that a whole generation of mothers experienced years of virtual confinement with their young children, or else guilt at leaving them for part of the day with someone else. A.S. Byatt has recalled the damaging effects of the idea that mothers should be with their children all the time, and has spoken with gratitude of Betty Friedan, whose book *The Feminine Mystique* (1963) encouraged women to work.[5]

4. e.g. E. Maccoby and C. Jacklin, *The Psychology of Sex Differences* (Stanford, Stanford University Press, 1974), cited by Mary Evans in *The Woman Question. Readings on the Subordination of Women*, (Fontana, 1982), p. 21.
5. Janet Todd, ed., *Women Writers Talking* (New York, Holmes & Meier, 1983), p. 189, interviewed by Juliet Dusinberre.

Feminists see the provision of nursery care for children as important in relieving women who choose motherhood of some of the burden of child-rearing, and protecting mothers' access to employment.

It is a reasonable criticism that in its early stages the women's movement paid rather little attention to the subject of mothering, and thereby limited its attractiveness to many women who saw rearing their children as a positive and largely pleasurable activity. The work of Chodorow and of Adrienne Rich during the 1970s has done much to redress the balance by reclaiming motherhood and incorporating it in feminist thinking.[6] The majority of the novelists considered in this study are mothers. Some, like Margaret Drabble and Sara Maitland, have stressed the importance of motherhood to them, and aspects of maternal experience form a significant subject in contemporary women's writing.

Feminist discussion has placed emphasis on women's right to a self-defined sexuality. For some women this means simply that their sexuality should not be defined in terms of dependency on a partner; for others refusal of marriage is a necessary consequence of their position. Lesbianism has become much more visible, and some women see it as a desirable political stance, rather than simply a matter of personal preference. The belief that 'the personal is the political' leads them to see heterosexual intercourse as inseparable from the enactment of male power. Some of the most influential figures in feminist theory are publicly committed to lesbianism – Mary Daly and Adrienne Rich are two of the most prominent. Literary treatments of lesbian experience are obviously not new, but in the climate of recent thinking love between women has become an important subject. The American writers Alice Walker, in The Color Purple (1983), and Lisa Alther, in Other Women (1984), have presented serious treatments of lesbian relationships, with a candour which was not available to Mary McCarthy when she wrote The Group in 1954. Among English novelists, Zoe Fairbairns and Sara Maitland both write about lesbian experience, in Benefits (1978) and Virgin Territory (1984), and perhaps the most striking testimony to a greater feeling of freedom is in the light touch with which Jeanette Winterson writes her comic first novel of 'Unnatural Passion', Oranges Are Not the Only Fruit (1985).[7]

---

6. Chodorow, The Reproduction of Mothering, and Adrienne Rich, Of Woman Born. Motherhood as Experience and Institution (Virago, 1979).
7. Jeanette Winterson, Oranges Are Not the Only Fruit, (Pandora, 1985).

Feminism and Literature

The application of new ideas about women to thinking about literature has produced extensive discussion both of how women have been represented in literature and also of how women write. Elaine Showalter traces the development of feminist criticism as beginning with a first stage in which 'images of women' attracted attention. This form of criticism has produced new perspectives and some reassessment of past literature, questioning stereotyped presentations of women, and considering manifestations of anti-feminism. It has been followed by a second stage of activity, the study of women's writing, to which Showalter applies the term gynocritics.[8] One component of gynocritics is the task of recovering a female literary tradition. Although feminist claims that women have been 'silenced' by men contain an element of exaggeration, and major women writers have been published, read, and admired for many years, it is nonetheless true that some aspects of women's creativity with language have been suppressed. Joanna Russ in *How To Suppress Women's Writing* (1983) has analysed ways in which women's writing has been disparaged, ranging from denying that the woman could have written the text in question, as notoriously in the case of the seventeenth-century English writer Margaret Cavendish, Duchess of Newcastle, to categorizing the work as inferior because it deals with female experience, or because it does not belong to an established genre.[9] For example, literature has been defined in such a way that some of the forms most available to women, such as journals and letters, have been little valued. In the creation of literary history, although women writers of truly outstanding stature, like Jane Austen, have had their achievement readily acknowledged, Showalter points out that many women writers of secondary importance have been quickly forgotten by scholars and critics in a way that does not happen with comparable male writers.[10] Even today, when bookshops are amply stocked with literature by women and about them, and with specialist material from feminist publishing houses, it is still the case that women's writing receives less critical attention than is given to men's writing. Women have commented on the fact that academic criticism of literature is very much dominated by men, who may find

8. Elaine Showalter, 'Feminist Criticism in the Wilderness', in Elaine Showalter, ed., *The New Feminist Criticism*, (Virago, 1986), p. 248.
9. Joanna Russ, *How To Suppress Women's Writing* (The Women's Press, 1983).
10. Elaine Showalter, *A Literature of Their Own* (Virago, new revised edition, 1982), p. 7.

female discourse strange to them, and may be unwilling or unable to do justice to female-authored texts. Male critics often react negatively to features of women's fiction, taking female modes of expression to be deviations from some obvious truth.

Gynocritics also includes theorizing about women's literary production. There has been much speculation on the question whether women have a way of writing which is intrinsically different from that of men. Fundamental to this is the discussion of whether women have a characteristically different way of using language. Virginia Woolf suggests that they have, when she argues that a problem facing women writers has been that the male sentence of the nineteenth century was 'unsuited for a woman's use'. A man's mind is too unlike a woman's, she says, for her to be able to adapt male patterns satisfactorily for her own writing.[11] Whether there is indeed a female sentence intrinsically different from the male sentence, as Woolf suggests, is doubtful, and has certainly not yet been shown. Woolf's own use of language is clearly different from that of the male writers she cites to illustrate the idea of the male sentence, like Johnson and Dickens, but repeatedly feminist commentators have concluded that the same structures that for Woolf are 'female' can be paralleled in male modernist writers.[12]

Dale Spender in *Man Made Language* draws attention to features of the English language which appear to be disadvantageous to women. Use of 'man' and 'he' as generic words for both male and female, as well as specific words for the male, makes women invisible. The naming of much of the world has been performed by men, so that names reflect male perspectives, and some things that belong to women have not been named. Words which are marked as female-specific are likely to have negative associations – spinster (as opposed to bachelor) and poetess (as opposed to poet) are two obvious examples.[13] Features like this establish that there is an element of sexism in the English language, but it remains to be seen how far, if at all, these limitations have significant effects on women's writing. The indisputable success that Jane Austen, for example, has in making language work for her suggests that women are able to find ways round any difficulties that may be inherent in the language. Gender must be placed alongside, for example,

11. Virginia Woolf, *A Room of One's Own* (Triad Grafton, 1977), ch. 4, p. 73.
12. See for example Toril Moi, *Sexual/Textual Politics: Feminist Literary Theory* (Methuen, New Accents, 1985), p. 155, and Sandra M. Gilbert and Susan Gubar, *No Man's Land. The Place of the Woman Writer in the Twentieth Century* volume 1, *The War of the Words* (New Haven and London, Yale University Press, 1988), pp. 229–31.
13. Dale Spender, *Man Made Language* (Routledge & Kegan Paul, second edition, 1985), pp. 14–24.

social class and cultural background, as one of a set of interacting factors that produce a woman's use of language, and it is at the least an over-simplification to suggest that women using words are working with a hostile medium. While there are certain areas of difficulty for women, some of the most accomplished writers take the view that language is, in many respects, androgynous. A.S. Byatt sees her literary ancestry as coming from Henry James through T.S. Eliot.[14] Margaret Drabble's writing displays clear debts to Wordsworth. 'You are what you eat', says Angela Carter, referring to the formation of her imagination, and the same is surely true of use of language. Some feminists would regard this as colonization of the female by the male, but such analysis proceeds from an unsatisfactorily narrow view of literary value.

Recent French feminist theory approaches the question of the nature of women's writing by making use of a blend of psychoanalysis and linguistics. French women point to what they consider to be crucial stages in a female child's acquisition of language. In the terms used by the French psychoanalyst Lacan, who has been a major influence, the child must move, as it develops, from the Imaginary Order, in which it experiences unity with its mother, to the Symbolic Order, in which it must accept the Law of the Father, and this is accomplished differently by female and by male children.[15] They argue that from that point onwards, the female uses language differently. Luce Irigaray speaks of women's discourse as having the characteristics of female sexual plea-sure, contrasting the unified, phallocentric experience of patriarchy with women's enjoyment which is diffused through genitals constituted from a number of different elements – 'her sex is composed of two lips which embrace continually'.[16] Corresponding to the multiple and dif-fused nature of women's sexual *jouissance*, women's discourse is fluid and not restricted by the rules that govern male expression. There is the powerful objection that by using such arguments Hélène Cixous and Irigaray are developing a new version of the biological determinism which has been so much criticized by the feminist work of recent decades. Their celebration of the diffuse, the irrational, and the mysterious comes dangerously close to being what Domna C. Stanton describes as 'a revalorization of traditional "feminine" stereotypes'.[17]

14. Todd, *Women Writers Talking*, p. 183.
15. Moi, *Sexual/Textual Politics*, pp. 99–100.
16. Luce Irigaray, 'Ce sexe qui n'en est pas un', in Elaine Marks and Isabelle de Court-ivron, ed., *New French Feminisms. An Anthology* (Harvester Press, 1981), p. 100.
17. Domna C Stanton, ' "Language and Revolution: The Franco-American Dis-connection", *The Future of Difference*', in Mary Eagleton, ed., *Feminist Literary Theory. A Reader* (Basil Blackwell, 1986), p. 237.

Some American critics have approached the question differently by asking whether aspects of the way in which females have been treated, or of the conditions in which they lead their lives, have a significant effect on the way that they write. Judith Kegan Gardiner makes use of the psychological work of Nancy Chodorow to propose that female identity is differently constructed from the identity of males, and that for women it is largely true to say that identity is process. In her view, there follow from this difference consequences for the way that women read and the way they write, and women are more likely to produce writing that is in some sense fluid. The woman writer may use her text as 'part of a continuing process involving her own self-definition and her empathic identification with her character', and she cites female use of switches through first, second and third persons in narration as an example of identifying with the creation while at the same time experiencing it as separate.[18] Certainly examples can readily be found of alternation between first- and third-person narrative voices, as in Margaret Drabble's *The Waterfall*, Angela Carter's *Nights at the Circus*, and Fay Weldon's *Praxis*, all of which suggest complex relationships between author and text, but whether these are specific to female identity, and significantly different from switches of voice in male-authored texts, is difficult to establish.

Elaine Showalter sees the specific characteristics of women's writing not in relation to their bodies or their infantile psychological development, but rather as arising out of the conditions in which they are socialized, and the nature of their experience. Women constitute a cultural group that exists within a wider culture, so that bonds between women are seen as coexisting with women's connections with men. She uses an anthropological model to explain her conception of women as a *muted group* 'the boundaries of whose culture overlap with, but are not wholly contained by, the *dominant (male) group*'. Thus there exists a large area of common experience between the two groups, but there is also a 'no man's land' or 'wild zone' which stands for aspects of female experience exclusive to women, and a corresponding male area which is outside women's experience. Women know what the male territory is like, although they have not seen it, because it 'becomes the subject of legend', but men do not know what is in the female 'wild zone', because the general circulation of ideas has been controlled by men, and men

18. Judith Kegan Gardiner, 'On Female Identity and Writing by Women' in Elizabeth Abel ed., *Writing and Sexual Difference* (Chicago and London, Chicago University Press, 1982), pp. 177–92.

either think that female experience lacks value, or else they simply do not recognize that it exists.[19] As women acquire both confidence and easier access to publication, female ways of thinking and feeling gain wider currency. Showalter, distancing herself from radical separatists, wishes to see women's writing as ' "a double-voiced discourse" that always embodies the social, literary, and cultural heritages of both the muted and the dominant'. Her moderate approach is very much in tune with the work of the English novelists discussed in this study.

Contemporary Women's Writing

The growth of writing by and about women has been a conspicuous feature of British culture in the 1970s and 1980s. The establishment of publishing houses that specialize in women's writing has made a significant contribution to this, and mainstream publishers have also been developing women's lists, acknowledging the existence of a demand for woman-centred material. Virago, the first feminist publishing house in Britain, set up in 1973, began by concentrating on non-fiction, and has been strong in biography and social history. It went on to develop the Virago Modern Classics series, thus putting into wide circulation work by many unjustly neglected nineteenth- and earlier twentieth-century writers, and helping to restore the female literary tradition. The Virago list also includes poetry and contemporary fiction. The Women's Press, which began with five reprints in 1978, has expanded to deal with biography, feminist theory, art, and contemporary fiction, as well as producing reference books on material dealing with women. Between them Virago and The Women's Press have made available, in addition to women's writing by British authors, texts from many other countries. They have also provided space for lesbian writing and for work by black and Asian women. Both presses are inclined to question traditional thinking, to be conscious of offering an alternative to a literary establishment formed by white middle-class males. Together they have done much to create a sense that women's writing, and writing about women, are lively and interesting and form an essential component of contemporary culture.

Women novelists today, whether or not they are feminists, and irrespective of whether they write for feminist publishers, are working in a context of increased activity and new possibilities. Their contributions

19. *The New Feminist Criticism*, p. 262.

to contemporary fiction are richly varied. Rebecca West suggested in 1974 that contemporary women writers, collectively, were over-preoccupied with the perception that for women the sexual life is largely a source of pain and insecurity. 'It is as if one heard a massed female choir singing . . . "how could you use a poor maiden so?" '[20] She draws attention to recurrent treatments of a paradoxical situation in which women seem to lose more by the absence of their lovers than they ever gained by their presence. Even in 1974, West's account was a selective one, and although she justifies her point with illustrations from Doris Lessing, Margaret Drabble and others, there were even then plentiful examples of women's writing that ventures into territory beyond personal emotional distress. In the years since 1974 many more novelists have begun to write, and others have produced more mature work. The women's writing of the 1970s and 1980s bears little resemblance to West's characterization. Although the heroines of Anita Brookner's novels continue to suffer the pains of insecurity and rejection, there are many other possible positions to choose from. Women writers are not all preoccupied with the personal life: many of them are interested in large-scale social or intellectual questions. They are not always satisfied with the world as they see it but their dissatisfactions are frequently recorded in positive ways, not in the form of simple regret. And in many cases there is a real sense of enjoyment of the possibilities of life.

In the final chapter of *A Literature of Their Own*, in which she discusses (in 1978) contemporary British women's writing, Elaine Showalter recalls Elizabeth Hardwick's argument, formulated in the 1950s, that women writers would always be limited, by comparison with men, because they 'have much less experience of life than a man'. She lists examples of experiences out of which great literature has been made, which have not been available to women, citing gross depravity in the work of Joyce, and terror encountered by Dostoevsky. There are several grounds on which Hardwick's argument can be challenged. Showalter points out her mistake in assuming in the first place that women are spared degradation and horrors. There is a further problem attached to her supposition that writers must have personally experienced at first hand what they write about. Novelists use a combination, in varying proportions, of what they have experienced, what they have discovered, and what they have imagined; Margaret Atwood has commented that with their skills in communication women are extremely good at finding things out, and so providing themselves with material.

20. Rebecca West, *The Times Literary Supplement* 26 July 1974, p. 779.

Angela Carter's work provides evidence that gender does not debar women from writing about a range of experience that includes the squalid and the terrifying. Taking the argument further, Showalter questions Hardwick's high valuation of violent male experience as material for literature, and reminds us that 'we are discovering how much of female experience has gone unexpressed; how few women, as Virginia Woolf said, have been able to tell the truth about the body, or the mind'.[21]

English women novelists in the last 20 years have done much to extend the range of fiction. Iris Murdoch, when interviewed in 1978 and asked about why she writes, when using first-person narration, as a male character rather than as a female one, replies very revealingly, 'I suppose it's a kind of comment on the unliberated position of women . . . .I think I want to write about things on the whole where it doesn't matter whether you're male or female, in which case you'd better be male, because a male represents ordinary human beings, unfortunately as things stand at the moment'.[22] Murdoch's analysis was correct when she made it, and despite the changes that have taken place since then it is not altogether out of date. Her judgement that it is therefore preferable to write from the standard position of a male is entirely reasonable, but the attitude she adopts is different from the attitudes of all the novelists considered in this study. A.S. Byatt is closest to Murdoch in being anxious to occupy an androgynous position with regard to most intellectual matters, and in her consciousness of herself as carrying on a tradition mediated to her by male authors. But Byatt adds to her gender-neutral approach to the life of the mind a breathtaking ability to conceptualize things about the life of the female body that have been almost inexpressible. All the other novelists discussed use, in some sense or another, a female standpoint. This does not mean that their range is limited. Alice Thomas Ellis, who is antipathetic to much of what feminists think and say, selects material which is in some ways traditionally female and domestic, but places this material in the context of theological good and evil. Anita Brookner and Margaret Drabble make contrasting assertions of the value of ordinary female experience. Drabble devotes close attention to women physically and emotionally in their relations with husbands or lovers and children; Brookner dissects the most undramatic, solitary female lives with similar acuteness.

21. Showalter, *A Literature of Their Own*, pp. 317–18.
22. Deborah Johnson, *Iris Murdoch* (Harvester Press, Key Women Writers, 1987), p. xii.

Drabble also quite explicitly rejoices in the opportunity to observe society in minute detail, and to chronicle a time of rapid change from a female standpoint. Fay Weldon and Pat Barker both have the boldness and honesty to lay bare areas of life that were once too painful to be looked at. Each of them is able to confront violence and to plumb depths that disprove Elizabeth Hardwick's opinion that a woman has less experience of life than a man. Together with Zoe Fairbairns they make the politics of being female a subject for fiction. Angela Carter, Emma Tennant, and Sara Maitland all move beyond realism and employ the power of imagination, fuelled by a rich cultural heritage, to produce penetrating diagnoses of problems from a female perspective, and to point toward new possibilities.

2

Versions of the Real

Contemporary Uses of Realism

During virtually the whole of the twentieth century so far, novelists and critics have been exploring ways of moving beyond the theory and procedures of the typical nineteenth-century novel, which has its basis in social realism. In the early years of the century, the great modernist practitioners of the English novel were discarding 'life-like' characters, the organization of incident into a plot with a clearly defined beginning and end, the chronological arrangement of events, and the use of reliable and omniscient narrators, as being no longer appropriate to their new perceptions of the world. The existence of an objective reality, which the writer described and a general readership would recognize, could no longer be assumed. Inner life took priority over external action and scene, and so ways of representing consciousness determined the ordering of fictional material. Yet the development of the English novel since Woolf and Joyce has not been simply a matter of building continuously on their work. English novelists have been distinguished from American and from other European writers by the extent to which, in spite of the radical innovations of the early years of the twentieth century, many of them have continued to write versions of the traditional realistic novel.

Since the 60s, English fiction has been moving in more than one direction. There has been a strain of vigorous experimentation, notably in the work of Iris Murdoch, Muriel Spark, Doris Lessing, and William Golding. The critical climate has come to favour fiction which acknowledges and builds on modernist principles, and some practitioners of experimental writing are inclined to dismiss realistic fiction as being naive and anachronistic. Nevertheless, there remain English novelists of considerable sophistication, like Angus Wilson, who see their artistic exemplars not among the masterpieces of modernism, but rather in the high achievement of the Victorian novel. David Lodge, who is both novelist and critic, suggests that the impulse to realism is an enduring one, and he points out that while we can no longer assume 'that there is a common phenomenal world . . . located where the private worlds that each individual creates and inhabits partially overlap', nevertheless most of us continue to live most of our lives *on the assumption that* the reality which realism imitates actually exists. 'It is this sense of reality which realism imitates'.[1] He observes that in fact the same argument over the merits of modernism and of realism has been taking place continuously throughout the century, and that the pendulum has been swinging so rapidly in recent years that all possible modes of working between the two extremes are now simultaneously available to a single generation of writers.[2] Significantly, writers who move beyond realism, and make use of symbol, myth and fantasy, often see realism and fantasy as being closely connected, rather than as mutually exclusive ways of writing. Emma Tennant, for example, who has had extensive experience of experimental writing, has nevertheless spoken of the traditional English novel as being the hardest thing of all to write, and something that is worth striving for.[3] Iris Murdoch places the highest value on the liberal nineteenth-century novel with its capacity to present 'real' people in a fully realized world. She finds moral worth in its concern to pay attention to the individual, and does not consider that this is invalidated by lack of consensus about what is 'real'. Looking in 1961 at current debate about what the novel should be like, she argues, 'Literature must always represent a battle between real people and images, and what it requires now is a much stronger and more complex conception of the former'.[4]

The three novelists considered in this chapter, Margaret Drabble, Anita Brookner and A.S. Byatt, have in common that like Murdoch they see the traditional novel as having the potential for further development. Margaret Drabble has become well known as an admirer of the Victorian realistic novel, who believes it can be adapted to be an

1. Lodge, *The Modes of Modern Writing. Metaphor, Metonymy, and the Typology of Modern Literature* (Edward Arnold, 1977), p. 40; and *The Novelist at the Crossroads* (Routledge & Kegan Paul, 1971), p. 34.
2. Lodge, *The Modes of Modern Writing*, p. 52.
3. John Haffenden, *Novelists in Interview* (Methuen, 1985), p. 293–4.
4. Iris Murdoch, 'Against Dryness', *Encounter* 16 (January 1961), p. 20.

appropriate medium for a contemporary writer. Her use of realism is modified in some respects to produce a development of traditional fiction rather than replicas of nineteenth-century novels, but she has been quite explicit about her desire to continue an old tradition, rather than strive to be innovative. She has herself written a biographical and critical study of the early twentieth-century novelist Arnold Bennett, in which she makes clear her admiration for the traditional modes which he employed. Arguing in 1980 that the density of Bennett's portrayal of life shows the depth of his knowledge of ordinary people, she says, 'Arnold Bennett tells you things Virginia Woolf simply didn't know'.[5]

In the many interviews she has given over the years, Drabble is consistent in her respect for the traditional novel, and her desire to utilize its resources as the basis for her own work. She shows little interest in the argument that realism has outlived its usefulness, and points out that especially for women writers, life has changed suffi-ciently for an exploration of the implications of new ways of living, done in a basically realist manner, to be an appropriate kind of new fiction. 'I and most women are writing about things that have never been written about, really;' she has said.[6] 'The rules have changed, the balance of power has shifted, . . . I'm trying to find out where we are going'.[7] 'Part of me is obsessively interested in social documentation. Just saying what it is that is different'.[8] She does not claim that her explorations of contemporary experience are more than recordings of life as she sees it. Her justification, if any should be needed, is in a large readership who find that Drabble's subjective vision is accessible and significant to them.

Anita Brookner resembles Drabble in having a deep respect for the nineteenth-century novel, and an ability to re-use its procedures suc-cessfully, although she differs in that she is not greatly interested in social change, and concentrates more on timeless human emotions. Her first two novels are in part based on nineteenth-century French works, *A Start in Life* (1981) being indebted to Balzac's *Eugenie Grandet*, and *Providence* (1982) to Constant's *Adolphe*. Brookner's

5. Diana Cooper-Clark, 'Margaret Drabble: Cautious Feminist', *Atlantic Monthly* 246 (November 1980), p. 72.
6. Nancy Poland, 'Margaret Drabble: "There Must Be a Lot of People Like Me"', *Midwest Quarterly* 16 (1975), p. 263.
7. Cooper-Clark, *Atlantic Monthly* (November 1980), p 71.
8. Monica Lauritzen, 'The Contemporary Moment: An Interview with Margaret Drab-ble', in *Papers in Language and Literature Presented to Alvar Ellegård and Erik Frykman*, ed. Sven Bäckman and Göran Kjellmer (Gothenburg Studies in English 60, Gothenburg, 1985), p. 250.

fiction has aroused interest because of the skill with which she manipulates completely conventional methods, to produce novels which are unfashionable, but which have vitality and integrity.

A.S. Byatt resembles Drabble and Brookner in seeing the realism of the nineteenth century as offering her a basis from which she can move forward, although she is more concerned with theory than they are, and her attitudes owe something to her extensive interest in Iris Murdoch. She has found that Murdoch's notion of a battle in the novel between real people and images, or a tension between observing contingent experience and giving the fiction a significant pattern, is meaningful for her own practice as a writer.[9] She has also considered the question of realism and experiment in contemporary fiction more generally. She does not accept arguments that the 'nineteenth-century novel' is now anachronistic and invalid, and she points out that even in aggressively experimental fiction, a core realism is still present.[10] In her most recent novel, *Still Life* (1985), she puts into the mouth of a Cambridge scholar a version of a frequently expressed criticism of realist techniques: 'Art surely can't any longer be thought of as inventing people and giving them names and social backgrounds and amassing descriptions of clothes and houses and money and parties', and she allows her heroine's thoughts to trace the implications: 'one by one the lights were put out, Tolstoy, George Eliot, Jane Austen, dead detail'. (Ch. 18, p. 215) In a highly sophisticated way, Byatt writes novels which employ essentially realist methods, while placing within the fiction an authorial commentary which develops thoughts about the complexity of perceiving, naming and recording.

Margaret Drabble: Modifications of Realism. *The Waterfall* and *The Realms of Gold*

Drabble imposes on her fiction a shape which gives expression to her own view of a changing world. She prefers a sustained structure to devices that reflect fragmentation, and she aims at lucidity because she is anxious that her novels should not be limited to a highly educated readership. Nevertheless, her realism accommodates modifications which reflect something of contemporary uncertainty. Angus Wilson, whose own fiction Drabble greatly admires, and who comments with

9. Janet Todd, *Women Writers Talking*, (New York, Holmes & Meier, 1983), p. 182.
10. 'People in Paper Houses: Attitudes to "Realism" and "Experiment" in English Postwar Fiction' in Malcolm Bradbury and David Palmer, ed., *The Contemporary English Novel* (Edward Arnold, Stratford-Upon-Avon Studies 18, 1979), pp 19–41.

the insight derived from his own re-use of nineteenth-century conventions, has written about Drabble, 'She presses against the outer edges of the realistic mode with such respectful serious teasing . . . that the simple or the hasty or the prejudiced . . . see only her competence, sincerity and readability, and give only ordinary consideration to what we mistakenly class as ordinary work'.[11]

Drabble's earliest novels are relatively straightforward narratives of life as young women experience it. Her fifth novel, however, is considerably more adventurous. *The Waterfall* (1969) retains the lucidity which Drabble has always valued highly, but it shows a greater awareness of the complexity of experience and the difficulty of recording it adequately. It also contains a sharpened sense that the relationship between fiction and reality is a problematic one. It is a story of a young married woman, Jane Gray, separated from her husband, who gives birth to her second child alone except for the visiting midwife, and who following on the birth embarks on a love affair with her cousin's husband, James Otford. Drabble presents the story in alternating sections of first-person and third-person narration. The two voices record differently. The third-person narrative is a detached, fairly flat and factual account of events. The first-person narrative is more varied: as well as recording events, it contains a quantity of information about the heroine's background, and presents extensive reflection on her attitudes and situation. Whereas the third-person voice tells the story in chronological order, Jane in the first person looks back on her past actions, in the light of subsequent knowledge, thus adding an extra perspective. Crucially, the third-person narration, frequently used by narrators to convey a critical view of characters, and to add a degree of objectivity, is in this novel employed quite differently, in that it is subordinated to the first-person narrative. It is an attempt made by Jane to tell parts of her story, and she establishes in her first-person narration that what she has been writing in the third person is not altogether a true record of what happened. Through the combination of the two voices Drabble is able to present alternately Jane's selective account of events, which omits parts that she finds uncomfortable, and her later view in which corrections and judgements are made, and there is a fuller analysis of the extremes of anguish and terror that are part of love. The first-person voice occasionally contradicts itself, but is shown to be struggling for accuracy and is to be taken to be reliable.

11. Angus Wilson, 'A Man from the Midlands', *The Times Literary Supplement* 12 July 1974, p. 737.

There is a significant relationship, as Ellen Cronan Rose has indicated, between Drabble's use in this novel of the device of the protagonist writing about her experience and Doris Lessing's enormously influential *The Golden Notebook*, in which Anna Wulf fragments her life and arranges it in different notebooks, using fictional *alter egos* to treat aspects of her own experience.[12] Drabble also inserts into Jane's narrative exactly the reminders of the fictionality of the work that are favoured by post-modernist novelists: 'I had at one point thought of the idea of ending the narrative not so much with James's death as with his impotence: the little, twentieth-century death. (I feel ashamed, now, to have had so vicious a notion)'. (p. 238) In her later work she makes quite extensive use of this device, which has provoked some critical disapproval on the ground that it is excessively Victorian. But to use an obtrusive narrator to stress the fictionality of the work is not a naive Victorianism, and it is a strategy which Drabble uses in common with many of her contemporaries, both male and female.

The splitting of the narrative in *The Waterfall* between the two voices allows for the separate presentation of different aspects of Jane in a way that has affinities with other female-authored texts which reflect pressures on identity. Emma Tennant offers a more extreme manifestation of the division of the self, discussed in Chapter 4, in *The Bad Sister* (1978), a modern female version of the story of the double told in James Hogg's early nineteenth-century *The Private Memoirs and Confessions of a Justified Sinner*. Drabble in her treatment of Jane is creating something more manageable, which does not, like Tennant's narrative, venture into terror, violent death and the possibility of schizophrenia. The author has given her own view that Jane's condition is not pathological: 'Even Jane, who says at one point that she's schizoid, isn't'.[13] But Jane's voice expresses a continuing sense of dividedness: 'I was hoping that in the end I would manage to find some kind of unity. I seem to be no nearer to it'. (p. 207) Within the bounds of sanity, the Jane of the first-person voice is ready to plumb frightening depths. Her imagination is kindled by female experience as mediated through nineteenth-century fiction, and she shares with the reader a grim passion unfamiliar in male texts, which can be described, in Elaine Showalter's terminology, as coming from the 'wild zone' of female existence.

12. Ellen Cronan Rose, *The Novels of Margaret Drabble: Equivocal Figures* (Macmillan, 1980), pp. 58–9.
13. Nancy S. Hardin, 'An Interview with Margaret Drabble', *Contemporary Literature* 14 (1973), p. 282

Looking back on her experience, and at the story she has told about it, she exclaims about the inadequacy of the account – 'no sin, no weariness, no aching swollen untouchable breasts, no bleeding womb, but the pure flower of love itself, blossoming out of God knows what rottenness'. In attempting to replace the edited account with a true picture of the extent of her need, she draws on the desperation of passion as delineated in *Villette*: 'it was some foreign country to me, some Brussels of the mind'. She emphasizes the importance of sexual desire in a contrast between Charlotte Brontë's husband, 'the poor curate that had her and killed her', and the fictional hero 'she created and wept and longed for'. (p. 84) The same voice subverts conventional responses as it muses on Emma in bed with Mr Knightley: 'Sorrow awaited that woman: she would have done better to steal Frank Churchill, if she could'.(p. 58)

Water imagery used in both narrative voices unites the two versions of Jane. Her fatalism is presented in terms of being incapable of saving herself from drowning. Literally, in her frigidity she has feared the 'fatal moisture' of love until with James she drowns in a willing sea. The waterfall of the title is primarily a card trick performed by James, which is used as a metaphor for their sexual relationship, and is significantly placed in the narrative immediately before the account of Jane's first orgasmic experience. This passage, in which she is able to accept her situation, 'trembling, shuddering, quaking, drenched and drowned, down there at last in the water, not high in her lonely place' is the central focus of a network of images in which water suggests life and fertility. (p. 150) The introduction at the end of the lovers' relationship of a visit to a real waterfall, at Goredale Scar in the Pennines, foregrounds the issue of fictionality. The waterfall is an example of the sublime, and it is at the same time like and unlike the sublimity of their romantic passion. On the one hand it exists in the real world, whereas their love is a fiction. Yet as Drabble has pointed out, their love must correspond to true experience, 'otherwise why should anybody want to invent it'.[14]

After accomplishing a substantial exploration of female experience in her early work, Drabble in the 1970s moved away from her concentration on personal concerns and began to write novels that take a wider view of society. A basically realist approach to the external world is appropriate for this purpose, and, using third-person omniscient narration, she presents characters in detailed, life-like settings.

14. Hardin, *Contemporary Literature* (1973), p. 292.

But in certain ways she modifies the conventions of nineteenth-century realism, to produce fiction which is appropriate to twentieth-century minds. In particular, she uses strategies which enact not certainty, but very specifically uncertainty. Cynthia A. Davis has pointed out how in *The Realms of Gold* (1975) key images are used to establish parallels between characters, so that for example one of the main characters, David Ollerenshaw, who is a geologist observing a volcano, is connected with his cousin Janet Bird, by means of a crater image applied to the sea of wax left in her ash-tray after a dinner party. A network of such connections establishes relationship, but also radical differences in situation and in perspectives between the various characters linked by the crater images. The patterning is partial and tentative. Similarly, parallel scenes, as in the lives of the cousins Frances Ollerenshaw and Janet Bird, are used so as to play off different perspectives against each other. The relativity of perception is illustrated by the varying interpretations of characters and narrator: 'external reality exists, but its meaning depends on the observer. . . .'[15]

Unlike the nineteenth-century novel which is unified by a dominant succession of events, this is a narrative in which action is of only slight significance. An exploration of a body of ideas emerges through the counterpointing of parallels and contrasts, and the result is to convey a sense of relativism and fragmentation. *The Middle Ground* (1980) is even more emphatically a questioning fiction, and is virtually a plotless novel, constructed around a series of incidents which have some thematic connection but which reflect the arbitrariness of life, not causal connection.

Drabble: Novelist of Women's Experience

Drabble has a wide popular readership, and she has also, unlike the other female English novelists of her generation, been the object of a very large amount of attention from academic critics. She attracted interest initially because she produced several novels in rapid succession in the 1960s dealing with women's personal experience, a short time before this became a popular topic. Her first novels were appearing just as sociologists and journalists were beginning to see the problems of the 'housewife' as a significant subject, and before the

---

15. Cynthia A. Davis, 'Unfolding Form: Narrative Approach and Theme in *The Realms of Gold*', *Modern Language Quarterly* 40 (1979), p. 394.

development of the women's movement. Drabble's books about young women found a ready response particularly among a readership of women who had received more education than their mothers, and then experienced difficulty in adjusting to domestic life. Although it is not her sole preoccupation, she writes particularly well about the combination of women's pleasure in their children with resignation to the demanding work of caring for them. Simply by making women's everyday experience the subject of her fiction, and dealing with it fully and tangibly, Drabble was asserting the importance of such experience. From the sixth novel, *The Needle's Eye* (1972) onwards, she begins to examine wider issues, but the personal lives of women are still central, except in *The Ice Age* (1977), in which a male character is the dominant figure.

Drabble has been seen as a writer with a special capacity to write about the experience of motherhood. Aspects of maternity have been represented in literature through the centuries, but until recent years relatively few novelists were themselves mothers, and Drabble approaches the subject with first-hand access to insights that have not been available to men or to childless women. She has said that for her personally motherhood has been 'the greatest joy in the world', and she has a sharp awareness of the mixed delights and anxieties of parenthood.[16]

She reports freshly and directly. The relaxation of prohibitions about what may be said (which, in literary texts, owes something to pioneering work by Doris Lessing) allows her to recreate experience in vivid detail – as in her portrayal of Jane giving birth and afterwards in *The Waterfall*. Here the dampness, the bleeding, and the mess of the lying-in are essential to the portrayal of the complex interaction between Jane's physical and her emotional life. The vulnerability that accompanies the pleasures of having a child is prominent in her work. Much of the significance of *The Garrick Year* (1964) lies in the way that Emma, the heroine, finds that her dissatisfaction with her marriage becomes relatively unimportant when it is put into perspective by her daughter's narrow escape from drowning in the river Wye. In *The Millstone* (1965) the major interest is in the effect of motherhood on Rosamund's hitherto undeveloped emotional life. When her baby daughter is discovered to have a dangerous congenital heart defect, she confronts depths of experience previously unknown to her.

Nevertheless, for all the acuteness of Drabble's sensitivity to the

16. Cooper-Clark, *Atlantic Monthly* (November 1980), p. 74.

processes of bearing and caring for children, and the wide currency this has gained for her books among women who are themselves mothers, Drabble's writing is less dominated by maternity than her popular reputation might suggest. The dreadful commitment that accompanies motherhood is the major concern in *The Garrick Year* and *The Millstone*, and in both of these books the children are tangible presences. *Jerusalem the Golden* (1967) presents an interesting gamut of maternal activity at different stages of women's lives. In the novels that follow, although children are frequently present, there is sometimes surprisingly little awareness of them as characters. In *The Needle's Eye* the focus is on Rose's inner life, and her interaction with her children is not treated very extensively, in spite of the fact that the matter of their custody is of crucial importance in the plot. In *The Realms of Gold*, although the heroine Frances is a single mother of four children, they have a muted existence, and the book is really much more about Frances as a daughter than about her as a mother. The Drabble heroine quite frequently has a difficult relationship with her own mother: and the author has herself commented, when speaking of the pleasure of being a mother, that she sees being a daughter as a more difficult thing. Sometimes her portrayal of difficult mothers expresses a painful awareness of how life disappoints women, and their youthful potential is lost, as in *Jerusalem the Golden*, in which Clara finds old photographs and exercise books which prove that before her marriage her mother had had vitality and aspirations long since quenched.

Drabble and Feminism. *The Middle Ground*

A contemporary novelist writing seriously about female experience must inevitably pay attention to feminism. Drabble, in common with many English women born in the 30s and 40s, has an attitude to feminism which is best described by the word 'cautious'. She is also anxious to point out that feminism is not a discovery of the late 1960s, and she represents this in her fiction by the inclusion of female characters in their 50s who have a long record of feminist thinking and of professional activity, e.g. the mothers of Rosalind and Frances in *The Millstone* and *The Realms of Gold*. She wrote in 1972, for an entry in a reference book on the contemporary novel, that her books are concerned with 'privilege, justice and salvation', and that they are not directly concerned with feminism because 'my belief in justice for women is so basic that I never think of using it as a subject'. In a later edition, published in 1986, she declares that she still stands by this position.[17] Over the years Drabble has expressed an attitude to feminism which combines caution with a growing sympathy. In 1974 she says to Iris Rozencwajg about the women's movement, 'I just don't feel I need it myself'.[18] In 1984 she expresses to Monica Lauritzen a more positive view: 'I am very happy to be called a woman writer and I am very happy to be called a feminist novelist. The only problem with the latter description is that people tend not to notice anything else in one's work at all. They seize only on the feminist issues. But I certainly think that the background of a lot of my thought is feminist and always has been. My mother was a feminist in her day and still is'.[19]

Drabble's approach to everything is shaped by a distrust of facile solutions, and a belief that there are many reasons, of which gender is only one, that may prevent an individual from achieving happiness in life. She has a strong general social concern, which leads her to be critical of arguments that highlight women's problems and overlook a gap between the ideal and the real which exists for both sexes. She has explained to interviewers that while she does not have a religious commitment, she was taught at her Quaker school to look for 'a light of God in every man', and this has left her with an enduring passion for equality and fairness.[20] She has long been troubled by the fact that fate or providence gives people unequal chances in life. In the 1980s she has added to this a deep concern about those developments in British society that place a high value on enterprise and acquisitiveness, and have in her view undone a hard-won sense of responsibility for the less fortunate in society.

Drabble's ambiguous feelings about feminism are made a central focus in *The Middle Ground*, a novel which combines assessment of the condition of middle age with analysis of the social conditions of the late 70s. In this book, unusually, she makes feminism an explicit part of her subject matter. The main character, Kate Armstrong, is a figure ideally suited to the exploration of women's position in contemporary society, since she is a journalist dealing with current affairs, for whom

---

17. D.L. Kirkpatrick, ed., *Contemporary Novelists* (St James Press, fourth edition, 1986), p. 248
18. Iris Rosencwajg, 'Interview with Margaret Drabble', *Women's Studies* 6 (1979), p. 347.
19. Lauritzen, 'The Contemporary Moment: An Interview with Margaret Drabble', in *Papers in Language and Literature Presented to Alvar Ellegård and Erik Frykman*, pp. 254–5.
20. Hardin, *Contemporary Literature* (1973), p. 286.

'women's topics' have represented a large part of her stock-in-trade. Through Kate's personal life, her social circle, and her professional activities, Drabble produces a comprehensive survey of the contemporary circumstances of female existence, in which sexual politics is prominent. Kate has, with her characteristic flair for timing, made a reputation for writing 'new wave women's pieces' before they became fashionable, and has had considerable success, which inevitably calls to mind Drabble's own production of novels about the condition of women just before that became a widespread activity. The negative side of Kate's situation is that as the subject of women has become more fashionable, she has felt trapped and limited and indeed bored by it. She is alienated by some aspects of feminism – in particular a best-selling angry feminist novel is mentioned as having crystallized for her an awareness of her antagonism to the kind of feminism that refuses to recognize that men also have to do hard and dirty jobs. (The best-seller is identifiable, from its characterization of women's domestic labour as work with 'shit and string beans', as Marilyn French's *The Women's Room*.) At the beginning of the narrative she says to her friend Hugo Mainwaring that she is 'bloody sick of bloody women', although she adds, significantly, that they won't go away just because she has got sick of them. (p. 8) The topic of opportunities for women is pursued through Kate's activity in making a television film about the extent to which women's lives have been changed by the Sex Discrimination Act. What emerges is that for most of them, in a working-class area, nothing has changed, and furthermore that women are reluctant to say anything critical of men in front of a male producer and camera crew. The novel ends ambiguously and inconclusively, with Kate making preparations for a party which is both like and unlike Mrs Dalloway's party as depicted by Virginia Woolf, and in a mood that Drabble herself identifies as one of 'guarded optimism'.[21]

The Radiant Way (1987) confirms Drabble's concern for social justice as her major preoccupation. Set at the beginning of the 1980s, it is designed to survey British society, chronicling change, and noting differences between north and south. The central focus is on three women, in their mid-forties when the novel opens with a New Year's Eve party in 1979, who have been friends since they met almost 30 years earlier as Cambridge entrants. They are examples of a generation offered opportunity by the educational provisions of the 50s, brought from the margins of English society towards the centre. The book,

21. Cooper-Clark, *Atlantic Monthly* (November 1980), p. 75

which is long and detailed, and constructed with multiple centres of interest, pays some attention to their lives as women – notably to the psychiatrist, Liz Headleand, who has come to her Harley Street practice from an obscure background in a Northern town. Drabble charts her roles as mother and stepmother, as sister, and as daughter of a mother embittered by a hidden distress discovered only after her death. The narrative begins at the point when Liz learns that her husband is leaving her for another woman, and examines her movement towards independence of both husband and children in a condition of middle-aged calm. But women's personal lives form only a part of the concern of *The Radiant Way*. Through a gallery of characters, several of whom are professionally in touch with social and political trends, and have analytic skills, Drabble examines British society in the 1980s. She produces a picture of times which Liz describes as 'mad' because of polarization between rich and poor, policies of confrontation practised by both right and left, closures of industries, and withdrawal of educational provision. The author contemplates soberly the abrasive and divided character of contemporary life, and although the perspectives in the novel are female, her concerns are with problems that confront women and men together.

In her writing Drabble is stubborn in her insistence on recording what she sees, and is explicitly uninterested in producing fiction which embodies an ideology.[22] Her early books about the struggles of clever young women to find freedom and opportunity for self-realization, often in the teeth of restrictive assumptions about what women should expect from life, were welcomed by feminist critics, some of whom were working with the criterion that good novels are those that express correct attitudes to women's problems. Accordingly *The Millstone* was regarded by some readers as primarily a celebration of female independence, because of the way in which Drabble handles the story of a woman's life as a single parent. This is an over-simple response, since while Drabble certainly does assert Rosamond's strength, much of the emphasis of the book is on the extent to which she is made vulnerable by her devotion to her child – an affection which, while intellectually she recognizes it to be 'a bad investment', completely changes her priorities in life.(p. 172)

As her novels continued to appear it became clearer to readers that although Drabble is interested in women, she does not have a feminist political stance. Virginia K. Beards recognized in 1973 that she 'lacks

---

22. Cooper-Clark, *Atlantic Monthly* (November 1980), p. 70

the idealism that active feminist politics demands'.[23] Feminist critics were sadly disappointed with *The Needle's Eye* (1972), in which the heroine, Rose Vassiliou, aspires to Puritan virtues of sacrifice, and in the conclusion of the narrative is reconciled with her estranged husband, Christopher, because she is troubled by the fact that their separation deprives him of his right to association with his children. Monica Lauritzen Mannheimer, for example, expresses reservations about the behaviour of Rose Vassiliou. She finds *The Needle's Eye* a sad and defeatist novel, because Rose is motivated by self-sacrifice, rather than self-realization. Drabble herself has added a post-script to Mannheimer's article, which is very valuable because it offers direct access to the author's own thinking on these issues, and it illuminates not only this novel but much of her other work. Drabble explains that she herself does not regard the novel as defeatist or depressing, because it shows people in a continual state of effort. 'I have never had a very high expectation of happiness, I suppose, for it always seems to occur as a gift or a miracle, so I don't find it depressing that the characters in the novel don't seem to get much happiness out of life – why should they?'[24] She adds, 'one of the themes I was trying to explore was the possibility of living, today, without faith, a religious life.' She says of the characters, Rose and Simon, that they seek identity, rather than freedom or liberation:

> These concepts have little meaning for me. We are not free from our past, we are never free of the claims of others, and we ought not to wish to be. . . . It would be a mistake to underrate Rose's genuine sense of the religious life as a source of motivation in her, for I have tried to portray it as real rather than neurotic, satisfying rather than dull. It does, it is true, suppose a purpose: indeed it supposes the existence of God. But Rose, like Bunyan, is prepared to make a bet on the existence of God.[25]

A considerable amount of the critical response to Drabble's work has been shaped by a desire that women novelists should write from a feminist position, and she is therefore reproached by several critics because her fiction does not express a sufficiently feminist outlook. Ellen Cronan Rose, for example, speaks of Drabble having 'regressed' in *The Needle's Eye*, and, dissenting from the author's own conception

23.   Virginia K. Beards, 'Margaret Drabble: Novels of a Cautious Feminist', *Critique* 15 (1973), p. 35.
24.   Monica Lauritzen Mannheimer, 'The Search for Identity in Margaret Drabble's *The Needle's Eye*', *Dutch Quarterly Review of Anglo-American Letters* 5 (1975), p. 35
25.   Mannheimer, 'The Search for Identity in Margaret Grabble's *The Needle's Eye*', pp. 36–7.

of virtue, regrets that she does not share the outlook of feminist theologians like Mary Daly (rather inappropriately since Daly's early feminist work was only beginning to be available when Drabble was writing her book).[26] She finds fault with her for failing to give sufficient support to a critique of patriarchy, and wishes for her to produce in her next novel 'an unequivocally feminist blueprint'.[27] Elizabeth Fox-Genovese in a 1979 article in *Partisan Review* draws attention to an 'increasingly harsh repudiation of female being' in the novels. Where Fox-Genovese would wish there to be an awareness of female struggle, she sees a retreat into androgyny, signalled in sexually ambiguous aspects of Frances Wingate in *The Realms of Gold*, followed by the choice of a male focus in *The Ice Age*. For her the fiction emphasizes not so much feminist consciousness as a process of middle-class self-discovery, and she concludes that Drabble's achievement is limited because of its concentration on individual fulfilment, often obtained at the expense of other people.[28] Fox-Genovese is largely right about the characteristics of Drabble's heroines, for instance the self-satisfaction of Frances Wingate, although she assumes too readily that the author approves of these qualities. But, more fundamentally, there is an irreconcilable divergence of approach between critics like Rose and Fox-Genovese, who in their different ways wish the author to conduct an argument in sexual politics, and Drabble who clings to the objective of depicting life as she sees it, and whose feminism is never more than moderate. While there is much in the work of both critics that is perceptive, from the literary point of view (as opposed to the viewpoint of feminist theory) there is little value in a stance which finds fault with the author for not doing things which were not part of her intention. Drabble is very well aware of the critics who applaud when she portrays a strong, independent woman, and deplore novels which reveal unsisterly attitudes, or which end with a wife's reconciliation with her estranged husband. But she is quite untouched by such criticism. She makes plain in her own comments that her aim is to set down what she sees happening, as far as that can be done. The judgements incorporated in her observations are consistently informed by a general concern for social justice, not by radical feminism.

26. Rose, *The Novels of Margaret Drabble*, p. 91.
27. Rose, *The Novels of Margaret Drabble*, pp 123, 129.
28. Elizabeth Fox-Genovese, 'The Ambiguities of Female Identity: A Reading of the Novels of Margaret Drabble', *Partisan Review* 46 (1979), pp. 234–48.

Anita Brookner. *Providence* and *Hotel du Lac*

Anita Brookner resembles Drabble in making use of simple, traditional story-telling techniques to give form to women's everyday experience. She is actually less innovative than Drabble in her approach, and although she places a very high value on artistic form, her instincts are to produce the sort of art which is so lucid and apparently simple that it conceals the effort that has gone into its creation. She does not question the validity of these conventional procedures, and in her use of them she exhibits such powers of insight, organization, and control that critics tend to admire her almost against their will.

Her subject is more restricted than Drabble's, in that she has less interest in social change and concentrates more on the personal life. And she writes not about women dealing with children and husbands or lovers, but about women unhappily alone. Her typical heroines are women who seek love and do not find it. Characteristically they are deprived of emotional satisfaction by a malign combination of temperament and circumstances. Brookner is interested in the serious-minded, conscientious woman, whose story often involves her being disregarded by people who possess greater vitality or charm and who are careless in their handling of relationships. Like Drabble she addresses the unglamorous problem that the life of ordinary people is full of injustice and dissatisfaction. She acknowledges that the material of her fiction is to some extent related to her own personal experience: 'One has to use one's own life: one has no other material.'[29]

Brookner's attitude to contemporary feminism is detached and wary. She does not see herself as a feminist, although she expresses admiration for Fay Weldon: 'she cannot be fooled, I love that.' She also regards Germaine Greer as a very intelligent writer, and her radical feminist text, *The Female Eunuch*, as a fine book.[30] But she does not see in feminism any remedy for the problem that she understands best – the problem of wishing for things, such as affection and family life, that by chance have been denied. Her heroines have aspirations that cannot be satisfied, and so happiness eludes them, but they are unable to change their aspirations. She emphasizes their inability to look after themselves socially and emotionally in a world full of people less sensitive than themselves. She makes skilful use of irony to expose their false perceptions and self-delusion, as in *Providence*, in which Kitty Maule, a

29. Haffenden, *Novelists in Interview*, pp. 69–70.
30. Haffenden, *Novelists in Interview*, p. 72.

specialist in French literature, has quite reasonably, but mistakenly, come to believe that the medieval historian who has arranged to meet her in Paris to visit the church of St Denis is in love with her. When they dine together in Paris Kitty's elation is presented in conjunction with bleak indications from the narrator that she has misread his behaviour and that he is not sexually interested in her. Her misapprehension is dispelled only in the final scene, in which she goes to Maurice's house for dinner, and discovers, not only that he has not told her of his plans to move to Oxford, but also that one of her less intelligent students is with him, acting as hostess, and that while she has been unaware of this relationship, it has been well known to other people. The story is handled so as to make clear that Kitty has been wrong, and yet that her wrong perception was perfectly reasonable. At the end, distressed and humiliated, 'She had the impression of having been sent right back to the beginning of a game she thought she had been playing according to the rules'. (Ch. 15, p. 189) The text of Constant's novel *Adolphe*, on which she has been working with her students, and which deals with the miseries of disappointed love, is interwoven significantly with Kitty's own story.

Hotel du Lac, for which she was awarded the Booker prize in 1984, is typical of Brookner's best work both in subject and in treatment. It is the story of a romantic novelist, Edith Hope, who in a crisis of her life is spending some time alone at a Swiss hotel. Through the combination of Edith's personal difficulties and the nature of her work and its assumptions, Brookner is able to produce in a slender novel a concentrated study of ideas and feelings about love and marriage. The narrative has a dual focus. Edith is escaping from an 'apparently dreadful thing' which she has done, which is revealed to the reader, two-thirds through the story, as being that she changed her mind, while on the way to the Registrar's Office, about her decision to marry. While in this condition of temporary exile, waiting for embarrassment and displeasure to subside, she develops relationships with the handful of other visitors at the hotel. She is befriended by a mother and daughter, Iris and Jennifer Pusey, who initially fascinate her with their zest for life. Another guest, Mr Neville, makes her an offer of a marriage of convenience, which she is inclined to accept until, by accident, she sees Mr Neville silently leaving Jennifer Pusey's room in the early morning.

The story is a slight one, and Brookner handles it in such a way as to accentuate the tedium of a life filled with walks, cups of coffee, and observation of the weather. The interest of the novel is in the analysis of Edith's situation – her desire for love and marriage combined in the same relationship, and her inability either to achieve this, or to stop wishing for it. Edith's plight opens out into a more general probing of ideas about romantic love. She has been poised between her lover, David, who cannot offer her marriage, and Geoffrey, who offered her marriage, but for whom she felt no love. Out of the insecurity and jealousy inherent in her position as the mistress of a married man, she has accepted Geoffrey's offer of marriage, but she has seen just in time that she cannot compromise and settle for marriage without love. Edith's desire for love and marriage to go together is not shared by the other characters. Mr Neville, when offering her marriage, makes clear that he needs a wife, but that he does not love her and has no wish for her to love him. Although Mrs Pusey asserts that to her love means marriage, this is no more than a cliché, and her defence of what she calls the 'right values' in invalidated by her association with her daughter's sexual latitude. Edith's London neighbour, Penelope, also contrasts with her, in seeing men as 'conquests', and preferring a succession of short-lived friendships to a stable relationship. Edith's progress to fuller awareness of the real nature of the other characters is a major concern of the novel. Brookner accomplishes this economically through the ironic use of language which, for example, pinpoints the uncritical nature of her initial responses to the Pusey mother and daughter. Although Edith is normally extremely discriminating in matters of taste, she sees their showy appearance, in her lonely and vulnerable state, as 'charming', their energetic appetites as 'glorious' (Ch. 2, p. 33), and when bidden to join them for coffee she sits 'basking' in their self-esteem. (Ch. 3, p. 39)

Hotel du Lac is told in third-person omniscient narration, done mainly, although not exclusively, from Edith's point of view. Brookner records her inner life in such a way that her low-key, controlled approach to life is for the most part rendered sympathetic. She sees herself as having a kind of unfashionable integrity which distinguishes her from what she sees as the 'ultra-feminine' woman, typified in the Puseys, who pursues men and at the same time pursues a cult of herself. The narrative upholds this distinction, and shows Edith as being governed by conditioning which she is now unable to change. This is done comically through the extent to which she is preoccupied with speculation about Jennifer Pusey's age and prospects of marriage. Edith is conscious of her own disposition to prefer the company of men to that of women, so that she finds the predominance of female guests at the hotel oppressive. This preference is traced back to her mother, with whom she had a difficult relationship.

In her interaction with her fellow-guests Edith's mind registers impressions in a dignified, formal, slightly melancholy way, but the presentation of her character is expanded cleverly by means of a series of letters about events in the hotel which she writes to her lover, David, but which are never sent. The unsent letters in effect provide an element of first-person narration, and they add significantly to the presentation of Edith, and provide indications about the nature of her relationship with her lover, which would otherwise be only very tenuously present in the novel. She writes to him in a way which is unexpectedly vigorous and indeed hearty, and spiced with cheerful if dated colloquialisms – she distrusts 'the cut of Jennifer's jib' (Ch. 3, p. 47), and suspects that the woman who is unable to provide her aristocratic husband with an heir will be 'given her cards and told to vacate the premises'. (Ch. 6, p. 80) These letters add complexity to the portrayal of Edith. They are obviously written to entertain; they may be intended, because of the radical difference between their tone and Edith's private thoughts, to suggest that there is a brittle, artificial quality in her relationship with David, or they may be there quite simply to show that this apparently low-spirited woman has another side, brought out by her lover, which is robust and energetic.

Everything in the novel has some bearing on how women live their lives, and the nature of their relationship with men. The minor characters are mainly female and represent different modes of living, most of them being in some sense dependent on, or controlled by, men. There is a major antithesis between Edith and the Puseys, based both on the contrast between her fastidiousness and their vulgarity, and on the fact that she earns her own living whereas they are both supported in an extravagant style by the business acumen of the late Mr Pusey. Monica, the infertile wife, represents failure in the obligation to provide a husband with the heir he requires. The superannuated Mme de Bonneuil is the woman who has outlived her usefulness. She 'lives for her son', and spends her summers in the hotel and her winters in a *pension* in Lausanne, visited by the son once a month, because her daughter-in-law will not share a house with her. The characters and events of the novel are placed in a significant relationship to Edith's writing of romantic fiction, in which she engages with the problem of 'which behaviour most becomes a woman'. (Ch. 3, p. 40) Her neighbour Penelope, happily outgoing and successful in getting what she wants from life, believes that Edith writes about those pleasures that reality has denied her. This is an over-simple assessment, since Edith does in fact have a lover, but Penelope comes close to the truth. Edith has not achieved the loving marriage she desires, and as she explains to her agent just before she leaves London, she is writing for the unsuccessful. Her fiction is based on assumptions about women's happiness being bound up with success in 'getting the hero' – the same assumptions that lead the young Frederica at Cambridge in the 1950s, in A.S. Byatt's *Still Life*, to see marriage as 'the end of every good story'. Edith's own character and attitudes, influenced by the mother who preferred men to women, depend on a wish for love which is a more sophisticated version of the assumptions of her own fiction. In discussing the representation of desire in romantic fiction, Edith identifies the fable of the hare and the tortoise as the most potent myth of all, and in a brilliant application of the myth she explains that she is writing for 'the tortoise market'. In her books it is the mouse-like, unassuming girl who gets the hero: 'The tortoise wins every time. This is a lie, of course'. Although in real life it is the hare who wins, it is shrewd to write consoling fictions for tortoises, since as she points out, hares are in any case too busy to have time for reading. Furthermore, 'The facts of life are too terrible to go into my sort of fiction'. (Ch. 2, pp. 27–8) Brookner in her own fiction returns again and again to the undramatic but deeply painful facts of disappointment as women experience it. She admires Fay Weldon because she cannot be fooled, and she herself has a similar capacity for clear-sightedness. Her strength is in the scrupulous accuracy and elegance of her analysis of ordinary experience.

A.S. Byatt. *Still Life*

A.S. Byatt's first novel appeared in 1964; since then she has written three others, and a volume of short stories. The two most recent novels, *The Virgin in the Garden* (1978) and *Still Life* (1985), are designed to be part of a quartet, and are both long and very complex works of art. Byatt writes slowly, partly out of her concern to write well, and partly because for a considerable time she combined her activity as a novelist with academic work. Since 1984 she has been a full-time writer. Although she writes with extraordinary insight about many kinds of female experience, she is very resistant to being categorized as a woman writer, fearing that to separate women's writing from the rest of literature is to invite marginalization. As far as feminism is concerned, she sympathizes with many of its aims. She has said that she admires Betty Friedan, and that *The Feminine Mystique* was written for her generation, born in the 1930s, who had been brainwashed into thinking that a woman's place was at home bringing up children. She places a high value on work, and on independence. But she expresses strong reservations about feminist approaches to literature, saying that she distrusts feminist critics like, for example, the American Ellen Moers, author of *Literary Women* (1976), which argues for a female literary tradition. Byatt regards Moers's approach as mistaken because she sees her as misguidedly using literature as a source of interest in women. 'I'm interested in women anyway. Literature has always been my way out, my escape from the limitations of being female'.[31]

Byatt's practice as a critic of literature produces in her a very sharp consciousness of the nature of artistic activity, and of the theoretical questions that are generated by the study of fiction. Matters relating to the theory of art actually become part of the fabric of her novels, as for example in *Still Life*, in which ideas about how the human mind perceives things, and names them, and makes connections between them, constitute a prominent element in the text. An unfortunate 'lady novelist' in the book who is made to proclaim maladroitly that everything is now relative, and that our art forms *must* reflect the fragmented and subjective nature of our perception of the world, is firmly told by an expert on Western painting that things can only be relative to *something*, and that variation in perception 'does not mean that we cannot study the planets; only that we must also study the eye'. (Ch. 15, p. 177–8) Byatt suggests in her critical article 'People in Paper Houses' that 'realist narrative, in English, is not in itself either impossible or *déja-dit*'; she notes how Iris Murdoch in her later novels, by adopting formal Shakespearian plots and thereby liberating 'an imaginative space for reader and character to inhabit', produces valid new developments within realism.[32] Byatt's own practice similarly takes realism and extends its possibilities. She has said that she thinks the last great English writer in the novel is George Eliot, and that she began to think about *The Virgin in the Garden* when a student asked her why it was no longer possible to write a novel like *Middlemarch*. She is attracted by the sort of fiction that offers a large canvas and plenty of characters, which, she considers, enables the writer to enter into other people's beings instead of just mirroring her own.[33] But her

31. Todd, *Women Writers Talking*, p. 180.
32. Byatt, 'People in Paper Houses', pp. 25–6.
33. Todd, *Women Writers Talking* p. 188.

dense recreation of life is different from that of George Eliot, and is carefully judged and controlled so as to be appropriate to the awareness of the late twentieth century.

The Virgin in the Garden, published in 1978, is, as Juliet Dusinberre has noted, both realist and experimental at the same time – in Murdochian terms, it is about real people and also about images. It is a naturalistic fiction in the George Eliot style, indeed in being set carefully in Yorkshire where the author was brought up it is in a sense a study of provincial life, but it is at the same time a self-reflecting text. Far from offering naive versions of reality, Byatt works at a highly sophisticated level: she gives form to experience, and at the same time 'Her novel demands whether any form can define reality, or whether the real is a dark chaos which even the Word – and the Christian Logos is part of Byatt's reference – cannot record or control'.[34] It is an extremely ambitious book which looks back at a period of recent history, just before and including the coronation of Elizabeth II in 1953, the time at which Byatt was entering her own adult life. In the novel it is a time of personal development for her central characters, the sisters Stephanie and Frederica, and also it is a time nationally of excitement at the beginning of a new Elizabethan age. Byatt is intent on capturing experience accurately and analysing it. Appearances and sensations are noted with meticulous attention to nuances of detail. Beyond the level of representation of actuality, metaphor is an important resource for her, confirming themes and imparting coherence with a pattern of images, of blood and stone, flesh and grass. Byatt has explained something of how metaphor functions in her work: 'I think there is an order underlying language which one searched for endlessly, partly through metaphor. . . . I found that the material came together when the metaphors cohered. But language relates things as well as controlling them. When I wrote in *The Virgin* about Elizabeth and the red and white rose quartered in her face, which is a heraldic image from a poem about her, it made me think of hanging, drawing, and quartering. That was linked with the image of meat in the butcher's shop, one of the original germs of the novel, which led on to 'All flesh is grass', a primary theme in the book.'[35]

Although *The Virgin in the Garden* contains a wide array of characters, male as well as female, and several men are given extensive and very perceptive attention, there are features of the text that generate a

34. Juliet Dusinberre, 'Forms of Reality in A.S. Byatt's *The Virgin in the Garden*', *Critique* 24 (1982), p. 58.
35. Todd, *Women Writers Talking*, pp. 183, 191.

special interest in aspects of female being. Beyond the fact that the central focus is on the two sisters, there are levels of significance relating to the coronation of a queen in 1953, and the celebration of the occasion with a performance of a new Elizabethan play about the first Elizabeth, written by one of the characters and performed with Frederica in the role of the young Virgin Queen. Furthermore Byatt has commented, about the conception of the novel, that she wished to substitute a female mythology for a male one, by substituting birth and Renaissance for the Christian scheme of the dying God and resurrection. A bleak northern Easter is presented prominently in the book, during which Stephanie, who although she is to marry the curate Daniel is not a Christian, is shown experiencing a sense of alienation from the words and ideas of the traditional ritual.

The second novel of the projected quartet, *Still Life*, returns to the subject matter of the two sisters. It is a remarkably complex work of art which combines a searching exploration of alternative ways of life available to women with a consideration of problems of perception, and the related problem of how things are to be rendered in words. The novel follows the sisters through Frederica's time at Cambridge and Stephanie's experience of marriage to a curate and motherhood. The story of Frederica is a *Bildungsroman* which analyses skilfully her coming to terms with her background – finding herself in 'the common and difficult position of disliking the parts of the culture to which she felt she belonged rather more than those to which she felt antagonistic'. (Ch. 16, p. 182) She is greedy for experience of all kinds. Coming from a home permeated with puritan humanist values, she encounters people from contrasting backgrounds who have different priorities, she participates in debates about class and culture, and she recognizes the limitations of her education so far – that her skills are rooted in the specific, and that she needs to learn to give critical consideration to 'large words' like 'liberal' and 'human', and 'democratic'. (Ch. 16, p. 180) Her political horizons are to some extent extended by the crises of 1956 in Suez and Hungary, and through their impact on Frederica's consciousness Byatt chronicles significant stages in the history of the 1950s. A story of female development must take account of the particular problems presented by the current notions of femininity and of women's role in society. Despite her strong-mindedness, Frederica has not been able to avoid the conditioning about female expectations to which her generation has been subjected, and she is looking for a husband, believing that 'marriage was the end of every good story'. (Ch. 9, p. 127) She desires to be 'in love', and she is influenced, negatively, by (women) tutors who assume an opposition between sexuality and the life of the mind, who 'had no idea what it was to be a woman'. (Ch. 16, pp. 183–4) Her sexual progress is charted as she discovers men, and eventually, though temporarily, discovers love. Falling in love marks a movement away from the familiar: 'She loved a stranger. The world was larger than it had been'. (Ch. 18, p. 216) All this is related through a narrator who stands outside Frederica and makes clear that the clinical tone of the narration does not correspond to the rich, confusing, emotional nature of the young woman's actual experience: 'The language with which I might try to order Frederica's hectic and somewhat varied sexual life in 1954–5 was not available to Frederica then'. (Ch. 9, p. 126) The account of Frederica's development is done with a full awareness of her egotism and immaturity, but also with a sympathetic consciousness of the extra difficulties put in the way of a woman, like the battle to be taken seriously by men. Her story is not brought to a conclusion. She falls out of love, and at the end of the novel she has embarked on a new relationship, and has left Cambridge to work in journalism. The Prologue, set in 1980, suggests that in her forties she is a successful critic, and has been in and out of marriage but is once more Frederica Potter.

The story of Frederica's progress is interwoven with that of her sister Stephanie's life as a wife, and as mother of two small children. This part of the novel offers a magnificently sensitive and comprehensive and intellectually controlled treatment of female experiences large and small. The momentous experience of childbirth is presented with insight and power, and this is the more satisfying because it is placed in a sustained recreation of the whole experience of a clever woman dealing with domestic and nurturing roles. Near the end of the novel Stephanie dies, electrocuted in her kitchen by an unearthed refrigerator as she tries to rescue a frightened sparrow. *The Virgin in the Garden* is dedicated to Byatt's son who died at the age of 11, and *Still Life* to a woman who died in her early forties; in the depth of her fictional treatment of accident, loss and bereavement Byatt gives artistic form to things that verge on the unbearable. Stephanie's death, and the grief of her husband Daniel, form part of a major strand in the novel which contemplates human suffering. There is a topical reference, important as an example of unendurable distress, although it is treated briefly, to the death of Ann Maguire, a Belfast woman who in 1976 saw three of her children killed by a car containing an IRA gunman. After giving birth to another child whom she named after her dead daughter, Ann Maguire eventually took her own life. Extracts from Van Gogh's letters are incorporated into the text of the novel, because of what they have to say about perception, and Ann Maguire is linked by Byatt with Van Gogh's mother, who named her son Vincent after a dead infant born the year before. Byatt sets Stephanie's death in a tradition of thinking about mortality, without in any way minimizing the pain, by using as an epigraph the passage from Bede's Latin *Ecclesiastical History of the English People* in which the brevity of human life is illustrated by a sparrow flying into a lighted hall by one door and flying out at the other.

Over and above the concern with Frederica's formation and the study of loss focused on Stephanie, Byatt is also, and perhaps most fundamentally, concerned in *Still Life* with the related problems of perception and expression. The still life of the title is taken up in epigraphs from works by Proust and by the French theorist Foucault, and in thoughts and conversations that occur in the novel. Reflection on the topic is provoked by the clash between the terms 'still life' and '*nature morte*'. Professor Wijnnobel, the expert on art, suggests in concepts indebted to Freud that our fascination with still life may have to do with a desire for 'another version of the golden age – an impossible stasis, a world without desire and division'. (Ch. 15, p. 179) Alexander Wedderburn, who within the fiction is preoccupied with problems of perception and notation, focused especially on his work in writing a play about Van Gogh, meditates on the notion of still life, as he contemplates the beauty of a breakfast table. For him the contemplation of the objects encompasses the idea of the growing culture of the yoghurt, the breathing skins of the plums, the germ waiting inside the stone. Alexander's focus is on the difficulty of accurate description, the process of communicating exactly what is seen, by excluding unwanted alternatives, and on the inevitability, if one uses words, of sliding into metaphor – if words like flesh, bloom, cleft, are used literally of a plum, the mind cannot prevent metaphorical connections from forming around the words. This perception of the impossibility of finding a language that is strictly non-figurative is announced in the Prologue to the novel, in which, some 25 years after the main action, Alexander reflects how when he tried to write his play about Van Gogh in plain language, 'Metaphor lay coiled in the name sunflower'. (Prologue, p. 2) Alexander's experience echoes that of the narrator, which in turn connects with the experience of Byatt herself in writing the novel.[36] The narrator confides in the reader, towards the

36. Todd, *Women Writers Talking* p. 194.

end of the book, that she had wanted to write a novel 'as Williams said a poem should be: no ideas but in things'. But the notion of non-figurative expression had to be abandoned: 'even in the act of naming, we make metaphors'. (Ch. 27, pp. 301–2) Language bears evidence of an overwhelming human need to make comparisons. In the novel the preoccupation with seeing, and naming, is presented largely through Alexander's mental life, but also through Frederica and her brother Marcus, who like Alexander apprehend things by naming them and thus making themselves aware of distinctions. Their mode of perception is contrasted with that of, for example, Van Gogh, who saw things directly, without saying them. Alexander is troubled by the awareness that it was possible for Van Gogh to get nearer to the life of the plums than he ever could, reflecting that 'Both metaphor and naming in paint were different from these things in language'. (Ch. 17, p. 195) In addition to maintaining this theoretical debate within her text, Byatt records objects and experience meticulously and searchingly, using an exquisite refinement of perception. This is perhaps most remarkable in her account of Stephanie's experience of childbirth, in which she is able not only to record pure sensation but also to produce by the exercise of the imagination a visualization of inner space. But small things as well as large are captured in a novel which is a sustained and triumphant demonstration of the power of language to present ideas, characters, and also the external world.

Margaret Drabble and Anita Brookner choose to work in essentially traditional fictional forms, and they combine this conservative approach with a firm focus on a subject matter distinguished by its ordinariness. In doing so they are consciously disregarding a cultural climate which places a high value on new ideas and on artistic experimentation. At a time when there is much interest in women's capacity for achievement outside traditional areas of female activity, the work of Brookner, dealing as it does with personal problems which are familiar, and at least in part created by conventional expectations about relationships, is both restricted in range and thoroughly unfashionable. Nevertheless, the area she takes for her subject remains a significant part of human experience, and in her treatment of it she raises a contemporary issue concerning the extent to which women are, psychologically, free to change their lives. She explores her material with a sharp intelligence, and turns it into art by creating a perfect structure for her narratives, and executing them with ironic and elegant understatement. Margaret Drabble uses tradition in a more adventurous way, and her work is shaped by a positive attitude to living in a changing world. For her, everyday existence is more varied than it is for Brookner. She insists on the value of ordinary life, and even when she writes about women who have more than average professional success she is still interested in how much they have in common with their less successful sisters. At the same time, by bringing to the depiction of ordinary life a combination of sensitivity and intelligence, she has been able to break new ground in recording the complex nature of contemporary female experience, and in her later work she produces a substantial analysis of present-day society which gives due weight to women's perspectives. Brookner and Drabble are in a sense complementary in that Brookner has exceptional insight into the narrow and painful situation of unrealized potential, while Drabble's mature taste for a wide canvas enables her to capture the confusing variety of interests, pressures and obligations that crowd into a different kind of female life. A.S. Byatt approaches the writing of fiction differently, with a highly developed consciousness of theoretical issues, and an explicit concern with the nature of art. She subjects realist writing to careful critical enquiry, thus developing it for her own artistic purpose. A foundation in realist procedures allows her to exercise remarkable powers of perception, in creating a verbal version of the material world. A complex discussion of the limitations of words, and a penetrating analysis of the emotional and the moral life, are placed within this setting, producing fiction characterized by a combination of intellectual rigour and a passionate interest in the depth and richness of human experience.

3

Fiction and Sexual Politics

Personal and Political

The concept that 'the personal is the political' has been crucial in feminist analysis of all areas of experience, and for some women writers the consequence of this insight is the production of fiction consciously shaped by their concern with sexual politics. Traditionally, at least in theory, fiction with an overtly political agenda has been named propaganda, and accordingly has been seen as having less literary value than texts which are free of polemical intention. For many contemporary women this distinction is open to challenge. Sara Maitland, whose own work is discussed in Chapter 4, has addressed this issue in her contribution to Michelene Wandor's *On Gender and Writing*, charting her own development under the title 'A Feminist Writer's Progress'. She explains that feminism provided her with a subject matter, but forced her also to confront a problem: she 'could hear all her old education and all her old artistic friends, and her own old artistic consciousness booming out that politics and great writing cannot go together; that gender and imagination are enemies not friends. . . . Inspiration, these voices hissed at her, will not be held captive to a theory, to an isolated vision, to a message. Feminism, though all very nice in its own way . . . cannot be Art.'[1] Maitland sees this problem figuratively as the negotiation of a dangerous passage between two grinding rocks – between on the one side the accusation that feminism cannot be art, and on the

---

1. 'A Feminist Writer's Progress', in Michelene Wandor, ed., *On Gender and Writing* (Pandora Press, 1983), p. 19.

other the contrary complaint that the fiction created by the feminist writer is not good feminism or is not sufficiently accessible to 'ordinary women'. Maitland found her way to deal with this problem through the formation of a Feminist Writers' Group, in which she worked with Zoe Fairbairns, Valerie Miner, Michèle Roberts and Michelene Wandor to produce a book of stories, *Tales I Tell My Mother* (1978). In such a group women who care both about art and about feminism can support each other, and Maitland stresses the importance for the feminist writer of such support – 'she did not just want companions on her quest, she actually needed them'.[2]

Tales I Tell My Mother is a collection of short stories, arranged to form a coherent work and combined with essays in which the members of the group pursue ideas about the relationship that exists for them between feminism and writing. They explain that for them writing stories is activism, and that they are attempting to reclaim femininity from the numbing and sentimental notions of the feminine routinely purveyed by 'women's' magazines and novels.[3] Sara Maitland, speaking for the group, defends their production of polemical fiction. She explains their aim as being 'to create a microcosm sufficiently satisfying for the reader to want to consent to it', and 'to beguile the reader into agreeing that this is how things are (or were or could be)'. Thus the story helps to make meaning of a reader's personal experience, and as she correctly points out, insofar as the reception of all art involves interaction between the experience of artist and audience, it is in a sense fair to describe all art as political.[4] The real difference, then, is not between art which is political and art which is not; the distinction which it is valid to make has to do with the explicitness of the political content: with the degree of prominence given to the ideas and the urgency with which they are advanced. The Feminist Writers' Group produce in their *Tales* stories in which the feminist politics are consciously accentuated.

They start with an acute awareness that they are writing in a time of change, and they see part of their task as being to document, for example, what happens when women who are asserting a new personal independence come up against people and situations hostile to the 'new woman'. Some of the stories focus on practical issues. Michèle Roberts's 'Womb with a View' makes real and undeniable the situation

2. 'A Feminist Writer's Progress', p. 20.
3. The Feminist Writers' Group, *Tales I Tell My Mother* (Journeyman Press, 1978), p. 61.
4. *Tales I Tell My Mother*, p. 114.

of mothers working part-time in poor conditions, who hesitate to accept an invitation from better-educated, childless women to come to a meeting about forming a union. Zoe Fairbairns's 'Acts of Violence' shows something of the complexity of arguments about abortion. Other stories have a stronger theoretical bias, and are written to demonstrate ways in which feminist consciousness has become, for the writers, part of their daily lives. Michelene Wandor's 'Keep It Clean' pursues the economics of housework. Sara Maitland creates in 'After the Ball' a situation in which she can examine aspects of lesbian relationship and biological determinism. The stories vary in the degree to which argument is embedded in character and incident, but for the most part the writers succeed in selecting and organizing experience into an artefact sufficiently satisfying to command the reader's imaginative consent. The volume is constructed with emphasis on the collective nature of the enterprise: the authors see themselves, despite personal disagreements on individual issues, as being engaged in the clarification of a shared feminist experience.

Zoe Fairbairns: A Feminist Dystopia. *Benefits.*

Zoe Fairbairns's novel *Benefits*, which appeared the year after the collaborative volume of stories, carries an acknowledgement that it would not even have been started without the support and encouragement she received from the other four members of the group. She is skilled in adapting forms of genre fiction for feminist purposes, and in her later novels *Stand We At Last* (1983) and *Closing* (1987) she takes the women's historical saga and the contemporary power saga and marks them with her feminist consciousness. *Benefits* is a dystopia which owes something to the vision of life in a totalitarian dictatorship in George Orwell's *Nineteen Eighty Four*. It begins with historical events of the year 1976, and moves into the future, spanning the last quarter of the twentieth century, a time in which Britain is seen as the arena of savage developments in a conflict between the women's movement and repressive political forces. It is divided into three chronological sections: the first, set in 1976, makes use of issues current at that date as a basis for projections into the future. The second part is concerned with the evolution of affairs between 1984 and 1991, and the final and most extensive part takes place as the year 2000 approaches. Over the 25 years economic decline exacerbates the conflict between already irreconcilable forces within society, and the novel is truly nightmarish in its projected view of a future in which women's lives are controlled by a state that sees their function as essentially reproductive and domestic.

Benefits is centrally concerned with women's autonomy, and this is treated particularly in relation to their fertility, which is the major factor that makes them vulnerable to dependency on and control by men. The twin issues of 1976 which form the novel's centre are control of fertility (topical because a select committee of MPs was considering the availability of abortion, and feminists were defending a woman's right to choose whether or not to proceed with a pregnancy) and the payment of child benefit to mothers. In the historical situation the proposal to improve child benefit highlighted a conflict between men and women, because it was to require a higher level of taxation, and the (male-dominated) trade union movement saw lower taxes as preferable. Women's reactions to this, which are represented in Part One of the novel, were mixed. In particular, feminists tended to be doubtful about the idea of paying women to stay at home and have children. But the conjunction of the two issues was clearly inflammatory, in that at the same time women would find it harder to escape from unwanted pregnancy, and would be denied the expected small improvement in the financial benefits that should support them in the task of mothering. One of the major themes developed in the novel is that if women are dependent on benefits paid to them in return for their work as mothers, this makes them vulnerable to having their benefit withdrawn if their way of life does not meet with official approval. Part Three of the book focuses on a more extreme manifestation of the manipulation of women, the 'Europop' project, which is to use Britain as a laboratory for an experiment to see how far total planning of population is possible. Plans are made at an international conference of males of all colours and political outlooks, 'all convinced (in this year 2000) that they represented humanity', to control the rate of reproduction by means of contraceptive drugs in the water supply. (ch. 6, p. 107) The results of the experiment are disastrous because the contraceptive chemical and its antidote are both safe in themselves, but when they come together in the water supply they combine to produce gross deformities in the children of women who subsequently become pregnant.

Fairbairns devises as her central character Lynn Byers, a journalist who at the age of 32 is having difficulty in deciding whether to become pregnant. She forms a convenient focus for the whole of the novel, because professionally she has a capacity to assess arguments with a degree of detachment, but she also has a personal involvement with the problems, more particularly because the child she does eventually have suffers from cystic fibrosis and so demands much more than the normal amount of maternal care. Lynn's profession allows her access to political events, so that she can conveniently and credibly stay near the centre of the debate in the novel. She also has a part in a strand of the fiction which considers issues about sexual orientation, because she develops a relationship with a lesbian feminist character, Marsha, which includes a sexual element.

Benefits is constructed as a survey of key events relating to these issues over a quarter of a century. The development of narrative is dependent not on a plot, but on the projected history of these problems, and on the phases of the debate. It follows that the realization of events and situations is highly selective, and the novel lacks, by design, the presentation in depth of individuals living through a period of time. Lynn Byers's progression into and through motherhood is not followed systematically. The situation of her family is examined at certain points which are significant because of thematic considerations. Mothering a child with a handicap affects Lynn's perceptions of the women's movement, which as she says is a bit short on emotional appeal for someone in her position. But her indifference is transformed to commitment when the government begins to withdraw benefit from 'unfit' mothers, and 'rehabilitate' them, and she joins in resistance. As Lynn's daughter grows up she takes on a new significance, because while her mother's sympathy for feminism increases, Jane reacts against it and joins the anti-feminist political party, Family.

Problems within the women's movement receive substantial analysis. Through Lynn's lesbian friends Marsha and Posy, who are in different ways influential participants in the movement, Fairbairns is able to draw attention to areas of difficulty for feminists. Posy sees as her life's work her attempt to find a unifying factor which will draw together middle-class career women from the United States and peasant women from the Third World, although as Fairbairns's narrative shows, it is not even possible for women subjected to the same pressures in the same city to come to a common mind on their most pressing problems. The tensions between the socialist feminists, the moderates, and the radicals, lesbians and separatists, are painfully in evidence. She also shows awareness of the problems that proceed from feminists' avoidance of hierarchy and indeed of structure in their deliberations, and of the problems that women wishing to live separately from men must encounter, in for example deciding whether their sons may be admitted to female territory.

Fairbairns boldly follows through the consequences of the way she has conceived her novel. The issues of sexual politics dictate the texture of the narrative, and a large part of the text is given over to forms of argument. Many of the events in the novel are political demonstrations, or electioneering activities, in which people are seen behaving as representatives of a position rather than as individuals. Much of the dialogue is political discussion. When characters reflect, it is likely to be on the politics and sociology of mothering and the domestic life, as in the thoughts that Lynn Byers has on the solitary Christmas Day when she opts out of the traditional obligation to cook dinner for her family. (ch. 5)

As a dystopia *Benefits* invites comparison with Margaret Atwood's *The Handmaid's Tale*, which deals with similar issues of sexual oppression in a totalitarian society. Fairbairns's novel is less satisfying as literature, because it does not have the sustained imaginative power of the extensively fictionalized new world that Atwood creates. But in the places where she has allowed herself to visualize the character of the resisting women's community in the tower block at Collindeane Tower, Fairbairns does produce a vital image of female community, as when she treats Marsha's arrival at the tower, exhausted after a long journey. (Ch. 4) The account focuses first on the external dereliction, after which Marsha enters a building which has structural faults but which is organized, although frugally, with imagination and consideration. Food is not only stored but grown – greens on roof and in window-boxes, mushrooms in dark cupboards. Space is allocated to cooking, to young children, to medical care. Holes in the walls are covered with rich tapestries. And a quiet, clean, comfortable room is provided, in which Marsha can sleep and restore herself: it is available because there is always someone who wants to be alone. By Sara Maitland's criterion of creating a world that beguiles the reader into agreeing that this is how things could be, Fairbairns has a large measure of success. Her nightmare vision of the future is very fully documented, and she shows remarkable perspicacity in that many of the issues she seizes on were much less prominent at the time when the book was written than they have become ten years later.

Pat Barker: Modified Realism. *Union Street* and *The Century's Daughter*

Pat Barker is basically a realist writer, choosing for her subject the lives of working-class women in the north-east of England, where she herself was brought up. She modifies her realism by excluding aspects of working-class life that might appear wholesome and attractive, and concentrating on an examination of poverty and the squalor and degradation that it engenders. By virtue of her unsentimental, unflinching depiction of hardship and humiliation, she creates what is effectively a political statement about the lives of women who have for all practical purposes been silenced. The novels provide a place where this group can be heard. In a BBC television programme devoted to her work she commented, as the camera showed women talking to each other in a drab street, that these women in their conversation are doing something similar to what a novelist does, by analysing character and event.[5] Contrary to popular belief, she argued, they are in fact highly articulate; the difficulty has been that no-one has been listening to them. Barker in writing her novels of working-class life has brought their experience to a wider audience, by displaying it and allowing it to speak for itself. Argument is not required, once the reader has been forced to pay attention to, for example, a scene in which a prostitute is beaten to death by a client, as Barker depicts it in *Blow Your House Down* (1984).

Her first novel, *Union Street* (1982), looks at first sight like a simple, almost transparent account of episodes in the lives of a series of women, arranged in ascending order of age. It deals in turn with the child raped at the age of eleven, the pregnant unmarried teenager, the wife of an unemployed husband giving birth to a third, unplanned child, and then with women dealing with the death of a husband, and arranging an illegal abortion for an under-age daughter. The narrative ends with the oldest of the characters choosing death from hypothermia in preference to life in what she sees as 'the Workhouse'. It is a version of the 'ages of woman', giving a remorseless view of the most distressing realities.

This apparently naive record is in fact coherently conceived and subtly organized. It is designed to make a statement about poverty. The degradations that accompany poverty are not peculiar to women, but Barker chooses to pay particular attention to the sufferings of the women of Union Street. The point about deprivation is made partly by means of detailed observation of substandard housing, inadequate food, and lack of privacy and facilities for elementary hygiene, but also, more tellingly, through the occasional flash of irony, as when Joanne Wilson, unintentionally pregnant and discussing the possibilities open to her, dismisses hot baths and gin: in the first place because it doesn't work, 'And in the second place, we haven't got a bath, you daft bugger'. (Ch. 2, p. 98)

5. *Bookmark*, BBC TV, January 1987.

As well as pointing to poverty, Barker draws attention to the amount of suffering caused to the women by their lacking the means to control their fertility. There is a repeated motif of unwanted pregnancy: Joanne's situation is shared by Liza Goddard whose husband is unemployed, and by Brenda King whose mother Iris arranges her illegal abortion. The historical perspective, provided through the characters' recollections, adds the gynaecological horrors of prolapsed wombs. The novel is preoccupied with 'birth, copulation, and death', with copulation being seen in the main as a manifestation of male oppression. Male sexual excitement is depicted frequently and coldly. Intercourse brings women little pleasure and leaves them lasting burdens – Iris King's summing-up, 'Five minutes pleasure and a lifetime of misery', expresses the attitude of many of them. (Ch. 5, p. 198) Although Iris's daughter Sheila responds, 'it's natural, isn't it', her voice is a lonely one and against it Barker marshalls the unwanted pregnancies, the reflection of the pregnant Joanne that lovemaking never brought her and her boy-friend any closer, and frequent unidentified glimpses of squalid, furtive couplings – 'white thighs and raised skirt' (Ch. 2, p. 101) – and bleak references to cold bums pressed against backyard walls while desire is satisfied.

Birth in the novel, as well as being related to the sex theme, is inextricably linked to death. The relation between the two is ironically highlighted in a grimly understated scene in which Iris King buries the body of her daughter's aborted baby, aware that she is burying her own flesh and blood. Young people come in the course of the book to understand mortality: the child Kelly, encountering Alice in her last few hours, and realizing that the old woman was once a child, finds it for the first time possible to believe in her own death. Richard Scaife, seeing the body of his dead father, knows as an inescapable fact that one day he too will die. 'Young though he was, he was the next in line'. (Ch. 4, p. 167)

The seven individual portraits are closely interdependent. The women's lives are linked because as well as living in the same street, and therefore knowing each other's affairs intimately, many of them work, or have worked, in the same cake factory. They share experience in the present, and in many cases also through past history. Muriel Scaife, whose husband dies, knows about the rape of the child Kelly with which the novel begins. Iris's daughter's aborted baby, which Iris buries in a heap of rubble in Chapter 5, is found by Kelly while she is playing, in the first chapter. At some points the characters' consciousnesses blend so that one woman is able to remember the experience of another as if it were her own. Thus Alice Bell in her last hours shares fragments of the consciousness of some of the younger women, and a sense of collective identity is established.

In *Blow Your House Down*, Barker continues the task of subjecting to thorough examination kinds of experience that are usually given little consideration. Here she writes about women living by prostitution at a time when a psychopathic murderer is choosing prostitutes as his victims, producing a fictional version of actual events of that time in the north of England, and showing women enduring lives of even greater horror and degradation than in *Union Street*. Her third novel, *The Century's Daughter* (1986), deals with the final stage in the life of an old woman, whose history sums up hardship and endurance in much the same way as did the collective experiences of the women of *Union Street*. Liza's story is told in conjunction with a narrative about the young homosexual social worker who tries to help her. As Lyn Pykett has noted, in a discussion of how women writers treat history, Barker uses realism, as nineteenth-century social novelists do, to confront and explore the individual's experience of family, the local community and the wider society. Her 'study of provincial life' becomes a vehicle for addressing the state of the nation. Pykett sees *The Century's Daughter* as being, among other things, a 'condition of England' novel, which examines the social and economic crises of the 80s through the perspective of other twentieth-century crises, most notably the 1930s.[6] She shows how Barker combines the close observation which is essential to realism with symbolic procedures which place the experience of the individual in a historical perspective. This is seen particularly in the use made of a painted metal box which has been passed down in Liza's family from her grandmother through her mother to Liza herself, and so becomes symbolic of matrilineal inheritance. The box is painted with dancing figures of women, and behind them are two other figures, one of a young man, the other of a figure that might be either male or female, shrouded in a long robe. The figures on the box enter the dreams of both Liza and the young social worker, Stephen. The dance becomes at the same time a dance of death for Liza and, for Stephen, a vision of disintegration and renewal.

It is important that for the young man the androgynous figure on the box unites features of Liza and of his father, thus creating a bridge between male and female. In Barker's first two novels, men are seen

---

6. Lyn Pykett, 'The Century's Daughters: Recent Women's Fiction and History', *Critical Quarterly* 29 (1987), p. 73.

mainly as callous or inadequate, whereas in *The Century's Daughter* some of the male characters are perceived more positively. It is a more complex novel, extending beyond her preoccupation with women's suffering mediated in part through men, and making more explicit her awareness that in the society she writes about, men treating women badly are themselves victims of social and economic oppression, suffering as a result of either harsh working conditions or else unemployment. They are not so much originators of oppression as agents through whom it is passed on.

Fay Weldon: Feminist Satire. *Down Among the Women*

Fay Weldon is now the author of 15 novels, as well as short stories and plays for stage and television. Like Margaret Drabble, she was writing about women before it became fashionable to do so, and she lets it be known that she had been thinking along feminist lines before the women's movement existed. She has explained that having been brought up in an all-female household of mother, grandmother and sister, after her parents separated, it simply did not occur to her that women should be dependent on men. Most of Weldon's work deals, incisively and devastatingly, with ways in which women are abused in a patriarchal society. Her basic weapon is satire. Since her first novel, *The Fat Woman's Joke*, appeared in 1967, her fiction has pointed, through a wide repertoire of genres, to the ways in which men exploit and belittle women, and women consent to this treatment. 'I have a campaign going, yes. It's at a point between feminism and psychoanalysis," she says. One strand in her 'campaign' is the need for self-knowledge, and the other is the condition of women. In her view, the world has been arranged so that it suits men: 'It's in women's interests to change the way the world is, and it's not in men's interests.' 'The difficulty for women is that they've been treated as if they were not people. One wishes women to join the human race.'[7] Weldon's stance is not one of simple hostility to men. She notes the weaknesses of women: she mentions, in discussion with John Haffenden, the tendency of women to lapse into 'the belief that you don't have to work and struggle because somebody will always be there to look after you', and comments that women have to fight as much against their own natures as against men's behaviour. In her view, the men in her novels are not worse than the women: she

---

7. John Haffenden, *Novelists in Interview* (Methuen, 1985), pp. 312–13.

suggests rather that it may *appear* to male readers that they are discriminated against simply because they are not given favourable treatment – an idea which is reminiscent of Virginia Woolf's remarks in *A Room of One's Own* about how women have served as looking-glasses 'possessing the magic and delicious power of reflecting the figure of man at twice its natural size'.[8] In the world of her novels men are typically selfish and unreasonable in the demands they make on wives and lovers, but it is equally true that the women consent to exploitation, because they are unwilling or unable to accept the challenge of independence.

Weldon is probably more successful than any other contemporary novelist at bridging the gap between the 'popular' and the 'serious'. Everything that she writes is lucid, in a sense 'simple', and totally accessible, and yet her work has substance. She has voiced things about women's lives that required to be said, and that have been welcomed by readers grateful to find in print what they could not put into words for themselves. Although her novels vary in content and approach, she typically uses a method of exaggeration and caricature, so that the behaviour of characters is preposterous and ridiculous, and yet sufficiently connected with what goes on in the real world to produce an analysis of actual problems. Her central focus is on personal relations between men and women, but she relates the personal to social change, and increasingly in her later novels she looks beyond marriage and the family to include wider issues. She writes usually about middle-class life, and her books emphasize that oppression of women, and even domestic violence, happen in comfortable as well as deprived homes. She employs a narrative voice which is intrusive and mannered, commenting on the behaviour of her characters, exclaiming over their fates, and using frequent aphoristic observations about the ways of women and men.

Weldon's second novel, *Down Among the Women* (1971), declares her theme in its title, which is used as a refrain throughout the book to emphasize women's low status and oppression. The principle that determines her choice of material here is that she focuses on the sexual lives of characters, and on the oppression of women which is inherent in, or produced by, their sexual relationships. The narration is divided between an omniscient third-person narrator, who puts events in a temporal perspective by reminding the reader of social and material developments which at the time of the story were still in the future, and

8. Virginia Woolf, *A Room of One's Own* (Triad Grafton, 1977), ch. 2, p. 35.

a first-person narrative voice which is eventually revealed as belonging to one of the characters, Jocelyn. The first-person voice guides responses to the text, by means of passages placed at the beginnings of most of the chapters, containing generalized reflection on what life is like 'down among the women'. She grieves 'for all the women in the world' (Ch. 8, p. 118), and expresses a mixture of reproach and self-accusation over the roles society obliges women to accept: 'The cleaner the house the angrier the lady. . . . Down among the women, we don't like chaos. We will crawl from our sickbeds to tidy and define. We live at floor level, washing and wiping. If we look upward, it's not towards the stars or the ineffable, it's to dust the tops of the windows. We have only ourselves to blame.' (Ch. 6, p. 83)

Characters and plot are selected to illustrate the argument about women. The central focus of the novel is a young woman, Scarlet, who like Drabble's Rosamund in *The Millstone* is pregnant as a result of a single act of intercourse, but who carries the consequent burden of unmarried motherhood very differently from Drabble's cerebral and withdrawn character, being at the same time more robust and less fortunate. After contracting a wildly unsuitable marriage to her mother's elderly boyfriend, she is divorced, and learns to live independently. Weldon organizes the narrative around two intersecting sets of characters: the histories of a group of Scarlet's friends and contemporaries allow her to explore the experience of the generation of women who came to maturity in the 1950s, and the contrasting relationships and attitudes of Scarlet, her mother Wanda, and her daughter Byzantia, create a historical perspective. Up to a point, what emerges is a study of woman as victim: men are arrogant, violent, inconsiderate or incompetent as lovers, and essentially selfish. But the novel shows woman as having, increasingly, alternatives to the role of helpless victim. When Audrey complains of her fate in being treated by her lover like a menial, Jocelyn reminds her, 'You did it. You chose it' (Ch. 13, p. 211), and in her function as narrator Jocelyn suggests that an evolutionary struggle may be taking place, and that, in the sense in which 'women' spend their time cleaning and being angry, 'We are the last of the women'. (Epilogue, p. 234) Byzantia, Scarlet's daughter, suggests the possibility of a new way of life when she questions the values of her mother's generation: ' "You amaze me", says Byzantia. "Fancy seeing success in terms of men" '. (Epilogue, p. 233)

Structurally the book is a series of episodes exhibiting aspects of sexual patternings. Weldon chooses vivid examples to show the absurd consequences of her characters' behaviour. Scarlet becomes

pregnant on the day of her father's second marriage, to a woman of his
daughter's age. Scarlet and her stepmother Susan then give birth in the
same week to children who are uncle and niece. This is treated in a
scene of bizarre comedy, in which Scarlet, already a week overdue,
visits her father's house to restore acquaintance with him, goes into
labour and gives birth in the bed prepared for the delivery of his new
wife, who therefore must go to hospital for her own confinement and
suffer inconvenience and neglect. Susan, the apparent winner, turns
out to be in reality no more fortunate than the displaced wife and
daughter, Wanda and Scarlet. She sits in a highly polished, glittering
world she has created, and 'none of it comforts her'. (Ch. 12, p. 193)
She does not really come to life until after the unexpected death of her
husband brings her independence. The consequence of being over-
dependent on men in emphasized in a grim second subject, in the story
of the beautiful Helen's love for the artist X. X's wife Y, also a talented
painter, kills herself because of her husband's infidelity. Helen in turn
takes her own life, together with that of her young daughter. 'What
kind of life is it for a girl?' she asks. (Ch. 13, p. 219) Helen's story is
treated with curt detachment; it acts as an example of extreme dependency, by comparison with which all the other characters are stronger
and more positive.

Much of the narration of *Down Among the Women* is done through
conversation, and there are frequent transitions between different pairs
of speakers pursuing the same theme, producing the effect of a chorus
of female voices enlarging on the topic of their oppression. The essential style which Weldon employs in all her writing is a concise one,
based on a high proportion of short sentences, and on the frequent use
of dramatically short paragraphs. The effect is clear-cut and incisive,
making for forceful statement of a theme rather than complex analysis.
'Style seems to me in the end a matter of economy', she has said; she
learned the effectiveness of concise expression when in her early years
she supported herself and a child by working in advertising.[9] This
conciseness is accompanied by expansiveness in the frequent repetition
of key ideas. The knowing voice of the narrator continually emphasizes
points, using generalized statement: 'A good woman knows that nature
is her enemy' (Ch. 5, p. 61) and 'There is nothing more glorious than to
be a young girl, and there is nothing worse than to have been one'.
(Ch. 1, p. 6)

Successive novels of the 1970s pursue the theme of what it is to be a

9. Haffenden, *Novelists in Interview*, p. 320.

woman in twentieth-century western society. *Female Friends* (1975) and *Praxis* (1978) go further back into the past than *Down Among the Women*, so as to produce a fuller chronicle of female development. *Female Friends* takes three women who possess representative qualities – Grace the man's woman, Marjorie who flourishes in the world of work, and Chloe who accepts a mothering role and cares for other women's children as well as her own – and follows their histories from childhood in a highly stylized narrative. The frequent reiteration of their names, 'Marjorie, Grace, and me', stresses the bonds that unite them through very diverse experience. In *Praxis* the heroine Patricia or Praxis has a similar, almost allegorical function of expressing the troubled life of woman, accumulating experiences as daughter of a mad mother, prostitute, wife and mother, lover, and eventually going to prison for having, out of a sense of sisterhood, killed the handicapped infant son of a friend, to release the child's mother from the responsibility of caring for him. Weldon's distrust of arguments about what is 'natural' is developed bleakly in this novel. As Praxis says, 'Nature does not know best, or if it does, it is on the man's side. Nature gives us painful periods, leucorrhoea, polyps, thrush, placenta praevia, headaches, cancer, and in the end death'. (Ch. 17, p. 147)

Weldon: Novels of the 1980s. *Puffball* and *Leader of the Band*

As she has developed as a novelist, Weldon has maintained her preoccupation with male selfishness and exploitation of the female, but other ideas have been combined with this essential theme. The novels become more varied, and she is increasingly inventive. She continues to write novels and short stories in the characteristic Weldon mode, but in addition she produces variations such as a fiction which incorporates a large amount of scientific fact (*Puffball*, 1980), a political crime thriller (*The President's Child*, 1982), an extravagant fantasy of female revenge on a deserting husband (*The Life and Loves of a She-Devil*, 1984), and a savage satire on militarism (*The Shrapnel Academy*, 1986). Possibly her most ambitious work so far is *Leader of the Band* (1988), in which she attempts a bridging between private and public worlds and mixes the erotic with an awareness of profound evil and suffering.

In *Puffball* Weldon casts a cynical eye on the differences between town and country ways of living, and considers aspects of sexuality and fertility. Her young middle-class city couple set up house in Somerset under Glastonbury Tor, and discover both the power of nature and the malevolence of the neighbouring farmer's wife, who is jealous of Liffey, the heroine, and constantly offers her food and herbal remedies she has prepared herself, hoping to do her harm. The marriage is threatened when the husband, thinking wrongly that the neighbour is the father of Liffey's child, leaves her just before she goes into labour, despite the fact that he has been far more culpably unfaithful than she. The novel integrates with a comic treatment of incompatible life-styles a serious consideration of the conditions, social and physical, in which women live. Weldon has suggested that she was exploring the idea that women are victims of their physical nature – an idea which in fact she does not agree with, and which, in the Freudian formulation that 'biology is destiny', feminists have challenged vigorously.[10] She exposes ironically Liffey's innocence and Richard's selfishness and callousness, but the marital relationship, while reasonably complex, is subsidiary to the study of pregnancy. Weldon stresses the blind, impersonal qualities of Nature, which she signals typographically by turning the initial capital N on its side. Nature for her is 'not God, nor anything which has intent, but the chance summation of evolutionary events. . . . Looking back, we think we perceive a purpose. But the perspective is faulty'. (p. 118) The importance of this blind force is represented in the text by substantial sections devoted to factual reporting of what is happening 'Inside Liffey'. The reader is presented with regular detailed information about her hormone balance, her statistical chances of becoming pregnant, and in due course the size and state of development of the foetus at various stages. The *placenta praevia* which endangers Liffey's life by causing a haemorrhage when she goes into labour is explained in similar medical detail. By chance Liffey survives, although in Richard's absence Mabs has refused to give her any assistance, and she returns home to look after her child happily and competently without appearing to care about the departure of her husband. When at the end of the novel he comes back she lets him in, but 'not without reluctance'. Although as Weldon says, she does not subscribe to the view that 'biology is destiny', she has produced in *Puffball* an extensive study of the power of the reproductive process, which changes the youthful carefree Liffey into a mature, independent woman.

The Life and Loves of a She-Devil is a black comic fantasy which takes the feelings of a scorned wife and exaggerates the possible consequences of acting upon these feelings. Weldon has always been prepared

10. Haffenden, *Novelists in Interview*, p. 307.

to face dark passions, and in this novel she depicts in a concentrated form the self-indulgence and self-delusion of the erring husband and the beautiful romantic novelist, Mary Fisher, for whom he deserts his large, ugly wife, Ruth. Ruth's remorseless plan for revenge, which is recorded in ingenious detail in the course of the narrative, provides an appropriate form for the rage of the injured wife. The book is a complex one in which initial sympathy for Ruth is modified or withdrawn when eventually she adopts the same system of values that motivated her husband and his lover, even to the extent having herself made smaller and prettier by a grotesque process of surgical reconstruction.

Weldon displays an increasing interest in public experience. In *The President's Child* (1982) the theme of conflict between male power and female power is combined with political allegory about American involvement in Europe, and in *The Shrapnel Academy* she moves further into political territory, producing a savage lampoon on militarism, which is driven towards a horrific conclusion. In *Leader of the Band* she proceeds further with the blending of ideas about personal experience and the public world, by focusing on a central character whose private situation has wider ramifications. Sandra Harris or Sorenson is a successful astronomer who at the age of forty-two leaves her barrister husband and runs away to France with a musician, mad Jack the trumpeter. She is pursued not only by her husband and the press, but also by 'History: personal, political, national'. (p. 2) She is haunted by ghosts more than ordinarily virulent, because her father was a Nazi war criminal and she is the offspring of a genetic experiment carried out on her gipsy mother. The narrative is slight in terms of incident: after a short, sexually ecstatic interlude, Sandra realizes that the fact that she and Jack have little in common will prevent their relationship from flourishing. She also discovers that after many years of remaining deliberately childless, she is now pregnant.

The familiar Weldon theme of men's inability to treat women fairly, and women's acceptance of this, is deployed again, this time with particular emphasis on the way in which Sandra outrages conventional notions about male superiority by being clever and successful. As her friend Alison says to her: 'not many men will marry a star.' (Ch. 12, p. 68) Sandra's husband says at the time of their marriage that he has no objection to her continuing with her 'little programme'. When she meets her lover Jack she disguises her position, next in line to the Astronomer Royal, as 'research assistant', and when the band find out, by recognizing a picture in an old newspaper, that she is 'Starlady Sandra', known to millions of television viewers, they are horrified.

Sandra herself goes to great pains to persuade Jack that a degree in astronomy is nothing, that the only people who watch her late at night are those who are half asleep in their chairs and too tired to switch off, that most of her programme is devoted to charts and diagrams, that she is just a passing presenter, and that what she earns she spends on clothes. Jack pretends to be asleep, but finally rouses himself to say, 'if I have to put up with your earning more than me, how about buying me a new trumpet in Bordeaux, so I don't have to mind so much'. (Ch. 12, pp. 67–8).

As Sandra tells the story of her love for Jack she is enthusiastic about conveying that what attracts her to Jack is sex, and how important her sexual enjoyment is, through, for instance, innuendo about the 'hardly innocent angle' at which he holds his trumpet. (Ch. 15, p. 92) The story of adultery is told with relish, this time from the point of view of the mistress who is complacent about her superiority, both physical and mental, to the wronged wife. Through the voice of Sandra, Weldon produces characteristic aphorisms about the nature of the sexual life, and of marriage: 'Women who play mother – who nurture, cosset, bite back harsh words – get left, as if they were the real things', and 'If you believe all you need is a man to make your life complete, that man will not turn up – or if he does, will stay for a night or so, and briskly depart.' (Ch. 17, p. 113)

There is a level at which Sandra's personal story has profound repercussions. She announces at the outset that she has run away with harpies and furies in pursuit, and in spite of her new-found sexual joy, these furies find spaces in her consciousness: 'no amount of fucking can stop you thinking'. (Ch. 15, p. 83) The reason that Sandra has until now strenuously prevented herself from having children, against her deepest inclinations, is that as the daughter of a Nazi war criminal she wishes to keep her genes to herself. Her inner life as she spends her time in France, largely waiting for Jack while the band plays, is filled with her recollections of her mad mother and brother, and the current state of her attempts to confront what her father had done. She thinks soberly about the nature of the genetic experiment of which she was a part, giving proper attention to the horror of it, but she also places these activities in the context of other applications of science, like the development of the atomic bomb, and contemporary forms of scientific interference with reproduction. Her resolution never to have a child herself is weakened, preparing the way for her reaction, in the closing paragraph of the main narrative, to the discovery of the pregnancy that she had not intended: she will allow this baby its passage into light, since it is so determined to get there. This decision is made rapidly but not frivolously: it is the fruit of Sandra's consideration of both the human capacity for monstrous behaviour and the need to respect life.

There are self-evident difficulties in combining accounts of genetic experimentation, madness, and suicide, with the depiction of Sandra's ecstatic middle-aged sexual delight. Weldon is skilled in handling the incongruities of human experience, but the disparities between the different elements in the fiction are significantly greater in *Leader of the Band* than in earlier novels. Part of the key to the reconciliation of the different kinds of material lies in the character of Sandra, and in the first-person narration. She is satisfactorily presented as a woman who comprehends within herself the ability to enjoy experience and to think deeply and uncomfortably, and the yoking together of violently differ-ent kinds of thought is established at the beginning of the novel, and developed so as to gradually introduce the reader to the full horrors of her background. Scientific metaphors act as a binding factor. The book also derives coherence from its essential conception which is that Sandra is facing and accepting the unsatisfactoriness of life. She moves from her early feeling that 'Our existence, if you pay it any attention, is unbearably distressing' (Ch. 5, p. 37), to the final position, expressed in Sandra's own fiction about her friend Jude, that 'What I marvel at now is how happy so many of us happen to be, so much of the time', in spite of the 'Great Universal Paradox' that what you want you can't have, and what you have you don't want. (III, 'Jude's Story', p. 186)

Weldon always produces narratives which are highly coloured and full of vitality. Everything is slightly larger than life, because she edits out the flat and the ordinary, to give the maximum impact to impres-sions which are nevertheless very recognizably derived from reality. She is a daring writer, willing to put into words things which are often uncomfortable and sometimes shocking, and eager to ridicule all kinds of self-deception and folly.

The argument that the imagination cannot be made the servant of a theory or an ideology is, as Sara Maitland has suggested, an over-simplification. Art may certainly fail because its ideological content is applied with a heavy hand, but Maitland argues convincingly for the possibility of an art clearly shaped by ideology, which offers the reader a way to make meaning of her/his personal experience, by creating a microcosm that is sufficiently beguiling. In very different ways Zoe Fairbairns, Pat Barker and Fay Weldon have found ways to satisfy the reader imaginatively, and to give artistic form to their ideas. Fairbairns's interest in *Benefits* is to give substance to an argument about social arrangements and the effects of their implementation on the individual. It is valid, indeed desirable, for a text of this nature to have a substantial theoretical content. Fairbairns brings to the subject considerable powers of analysis, and her use of the futuristic mode allows her imaginatively to develop ideas to disturbing conclusions. Barker approaches her subject quite differently. She applies a selective realism to the lives of an under-represented group, and is thus able to produce a powerful exposure of the extent to which some women suffer poverty, humiliation, and brutality. She produces fiction which is not greatly concerned with argument in the form of political concepts, but which creates a political reaction in the mind of any reader who pays attention to what she shows. Weldon has applied the techniques of the satirist, in a highly polished way, to recent and contemporary life. Her fictional arguments against male exploitation of women, and women's submission to second-class treatment, are made acceptable and effective by the wit with which she attacks complacency, hypocrisy, selfishness and laziness, and the sharpness with which her narrators analyse motivation and the connection between cause and effect.

4

Myths, Dreams and Nightmares

Beyond Everyday Reality

There are substantial areas of experience that are not best approached using the methods of social realism, and that require that the illusion of everyday reality should either be suspended, or never attempted at all. Fantasy, or magic realism, or contemporary Gothic, often overlapping within the work of the same author, allow writers to explore such areas. Angela Carter and Emma Tennant both write fiction which slides easily between the mimetic and the marvellous. Rosemary Jackson gives in *Fantasy: The Literature of Subversion* an accurate account of the procedures of fantastic narratives: 'They assert that what they are telling is real – relying on the conventions of realistic fiction to do so – and then they proceed to break that assumption of realism by introducing what, within these terms, is manifestly unreal'.[1] Carter and Tennant both write in this way. Each of them emphasizes that for her fantasy, insofar as it applies to her work, does not mean something whimsical, or created in a random or escapist way. Rather it indicates a mode in which dreams, or metaphors, are employed to say something about social and historical or psychological realities. Carter comments that 'there's a materiality to imaginative life and imaginative experience which should be taken quite seriously', and Tennant, asked whether she could be said to set up a fantasy life as a substitute for traditional plotting and characterization, replies: 'I never saw a fantasy

1. Rosemary Jackson, *Fantasy: the Literature of Subversion* (Methuen, New Accents, 1981), p. 34.

world. What I did was to stress what was going on inside people . . . and I did it often in metaphor.' So trees turn red or grey as reflections of the state of mind of the observer.[2] Both insist that they are not reaching towards some transcendent reality. Carter makes clear that she writes out of 'an absolute and committed materialism', a conviction that *'this* world is all that there is'.[3] Tennant rejects any suggestion that she might believe in a psychic or magic dimension to life, making plain that she actually fears what she describes as numinous ways of thinking, and insisting that the literal and the figurative can coexist but are not the same, and must be seen to be different.

David Punter has suggested that Gothic is a mode of writing which essentially questions, in varying degrees, the notion of the 'real'. Gothic writers may agree that in general the world is as realists perceive it to be, but think that at certain significant moments it is quite different, or they may question the whole notion of a real world, or adopt any of a variety of positions in between, but, 'At all events, the Gothic writer insists, realism is not the whole story: the world, at least in some aspects, is very much more inexplicable – or mysterious, or terrifying, or violent – than that.'[4] Carter and Tennant have some of this restless, questioning impulse that characterizes much of Gothic fiction. Punter also draws attention to the fact that many of the most important Gothic writers have been women (so that Carter and Tennant take their place in a tradition in which they follow Ann Radcliffe, Mary Shelley and Isak Dinesen) and that Gothic frequently addresses problems of dark aspects of sexuality. For Carter in particular, variations on Gothic have provided the medium for disturbing explorations of sexual violence in *Heroes and Villains* (1969) and *The Passion of New Eve* (1977).

Sara Maitland and Alice Thomas Ellis, who are also discussed in this chapter, are different from Carter and Tennant in being both committed to Christian belief, so that for them a move away from social realism reflects their interest in a reality that cannot be adequately expressed in terms that concentrate on the material. But Maitland has much in common with Carter and Tennant in that like them she is

2. John Haffenden, *Novelists in Interview* (Methuen, 1985), pp. 85, 294–5. My accounts of Angela Carter and Emma Tennant are generally indebted to Haffenden's interviews with them.
3. 'Notes From the Front Line', in Michelene Wandor, ed., *On Gender and Writing* (Pandora Press, 1983), p. 70. My account of Carter is generally indebted to this essay.
4. David Punter, *The Literature of Terror. A History of Gothic Fictions from 1765 to the Present Day* (Longman, 1980), pp. 407–11.

concerned with a critical scrutiny of myths. For a woman in the late twentieth century, traditional mythologies have many deficiencies attributable to their having been largely devised by men, so that they are frequently blind to the different situations and perspectives of women. Maitland is as much committed to feminism as Carter and Tennant, and all three are both thoroughly familiar with the culture of the past, and in some respects deeply critical of it. They make use of folklore, literature, classical mythology, and also the modern mythologies of Freud and Jung, in order to explore issues that affect them as women today. Alice Thomas Ellis, like the other three writers, blends elements of realist narrative with non-naturalistic material, and makes use of the resources of legend and fairy-tale, but she has a different, thoroughly traditional outlook and is indifferent, indeed in some ways hostile, to feminism.

Angela Carter's Early Work. *The Magic Toyshop*

Angela Carter is consciously a feminist writer, happily – unlike many women writers – accepting that designation, and saying that she is feminist in everything else and that one cannot compartmentalize one's life. She insists that the circumstances of women are different from those of men; that if one is female, just as if (in British society) one is black, one is aware that one's position is not the standard one; and that she is saying in her work that 'women are people too', a sentiment which closely resembles Fay Weldon's wish for women to be allowed to join the human race.[5] Carter traces much of her formation to the experiences of the 60s, recalling a sense of heightened awareness – 'truly, it felt like Year One', she says, and speaks of questioning the nature of reality, and the 'social fiction of my "femininity" ', which was created by means outside her control and palmed off on her as the real thing.[6] Although Carter is averse to didactic writing, as she makes clear in expressing a negative response to Marilyn French's feminist propagandist novel *The Women's Room*, her use of non-naturalistic narrative is applied to the development of a critique of psychological and social realities. She likens her activity to the eighteenth-century making of fictional societies that reflect on real society, and in her best work Carter creates a rich, concentrated exploration of human

5. 'Notes From the Front Line', p. 69, and Haffenden, *Novelists in Interview*, pp. 93–4.
6. 'Notes From the Front Line', p. 70.

experience. She sees her intellectual progress as being a kind of decolonization through which she has re-examined the version of reality presented to her by a patriarchal society, and rejected it. Sexuality is a central preoccupation: 'Since it was primarily through my sexual and emotional life that I was radicalized – that I first became truly aware of the difference between how I was and how I was expected to be – I found myself, as I grew older, increasingly writing about sexuality and its manifestations in human practice.'[7]

Already in her second novel, *The Magic Toyshop* (1967), completed before the radical thinking of the 60s had come to boiling point, she is, in Lorna Sage's phrase, 'turning myths inside out'.[8] The novel is described by its author as 'a malign fairy-tale'; it possesses fairy-tale qualities because despite being set in London in the second half of the twentieth century, it is only very tenuously located in place and time, and the narrative, being stripped of much of the detail that in more conventional fiction provides a sense of the real world, acquires a timeless and universal quality, the quality of significant drama being enacted 'once upon a time'. Carter uses an eclectic assortment of material from myth, fairy-tale and legend to tell a tale of patriarchal tyranny overthrown, from the perspective of an adolescent girl, Melanie, who with her brother and sister is subjected after the accidental deaths of their parents to the authority of her uncle, Philip. Melanie is poised between Philip and a contrasting male figure, her aunt Margaret's young brother Finn. In spite of initially seeming to her uncouth and distasteful, Finn represents a warm and vital sexuality and becomes her ally, protector, and ultimately sexual partner. Carter creates a dense fabric of reference interweaving various mythologies, through which she can develop a critique of Philip's male oppression. He is associated repeatedly with Jove, and connected with the rape of Europa, and with imagery of thunder. He is a toymaker and puppet-master, and his manipulation of Melanie culminates in an obscene puppet show of 'Leda and the Swan' in which she is forced to be 'mounted' by the swan he has created. He is further defined by fairy-tale references, e.g. to the closed doors, and the horrors of mutilation, in the house of Bluebeard. Carter adds to this her own re-working of the Christian myth of the Fortunate Fall, in which Melanie and Finn parallel Adam and Eve, not in the orthodox sense

---

7. 'Notes From the Front Line', p. 72.
8. Lorna Sage, 'The Savage Sideshow: A Profile of Angela Carter', in Ian Hamilton ed., *The New Review Anthology* (Paladin, 1987), p. 294.

that their fall allows for the possibility of redemption, but in the simple and subversive sense that they have quarrelled with a patriarchal figure like God the Father and it has been their good fortune to escape from him. He perishes in his own fire, and the young lovers escape and are left at the end of the novel, facing each other alone in a garden, like Adam and Eve after their expulsion from Eden and beginning a new life. Carter does not restrict herself to traditional mythologies: she also takes the modern patterns imposed on experience by Freud, and significantly modifies them. Freud discussed in his essay 'On the Uncanny' E.T.A. Hoffmann's story of puppet-master and puppet, 'The Sandman', and Paulina Palmer has drawn attention to the way in which Carter has adapted material from this analysis of the tale. She notes that whilst Freud foregrounds the male experience in Hoffmann's tale, interpreting it in terms of symbolic fears of castration, and marginalizes the female Olympia, Carter challenges Freud's priorities by foregrounding the female experience in her version of the story.[9]

The young man, Finn, is presented consistently with emphasis on sexuality and also on warmth and human feeling. References to Pan, a satyr, and a tawny lion poised for the kill, make clear his status as an icon of male physical vitality. Carter's treatment of this is complex. Initially Melanie is repelled by him and finds his attentions invasive, but eventually she enters voluntarily into a relationship with him. The pattern of symbols within the narrative consistently associates Finn with harmony, warmth, grace and energy. Melanie's initial distrust and distaste give way to grateful acceptance of all the 'red people', Finn and his brother Francie and her aunt Margaret, as kind protectors, who live brightly and vividly. To her they are 'three angels. . . . All the red people lighting a bonfire for her, to brighten away the wolves and tigers of this dreadful forest in which she lived'. (Ch. 6, p. 122) The colour symbolism consistently enforces the contrast between the vitality of the red-haired, musical, Irish Jowle family, into whose circle Melanie is glad to enter, and the colourless, cold authority of Philip. The novel begins and ends with a literary symbolism that conveys the excitement of sexual discovery through ideas about geographical exploration: at the end, Melanie and Finn face each other in the garden of the ruined house 'in a wild surmise', as did the explorers of the new America in Keats's 'On First Looking into Chapman's Homer'. The

9. Paulina Palmer, 'From "Coded Mannequin" to Bird Woman: Angela Carter's Magic Flight', in Sue Roe, ed., *Women Reading Women's Writing* (Harvester Press, 1987), p. 182 ff.

essential organization of the novel is based on contrasts between sexual relationships, which foreground the issue of power. Philip's abuse of Melanie by forcing her to mime submission to the puppet swan is vicariously an incestuous rape. The narrative condemns the coercive and violent aspects of Philip's behaviour, but on the other hand Carter challenges the incest taboo in her depiction of the serene sexual relationship between Margaret and her brother Francie: 'Like the Kings and Queens of Ancient Egypt'. (Ch. 9, p. 194) It is a challenging book, which refuses to simplify, or to disguise uncomfortable perceptions about the limited choices that may be available to women.

The symbols of puppet and puppeteer are used again in an exposure of male oppression and humiliation of the female in the story, 'The Loves of Lady Purple', in Carter's collection *Fireworks* (1974). She selected this story to reprint in her *Wayward Girls and Wicked Women* (1986), a collection of stories by women from different periods and cultures, connected by the fact that in all of them women adopt dominant roles. Her Lady Purple is a life-size female puppet who becomes the focus for the puppeteer's erotic and depersonalizing fantasies. When he speaks in her character his voice is 'a thick, lascivious murmur like fur soaked in honey'; he assures audiences that she is 'the petrification of a universal whore and had once been a woman in whom too much life had negated life itself, whose kisses had withered like acids and whose embrace blasted like lightning'. (pp. 257, 258) He creates around her a tissue of ideas of woman as torturer, as murderer, as source of disease, as nymphomaniac and necrophiliac. Carter uses the freedom permitted by fantasy to achieve revenge: as he kisses Lady Purple goodnight, the puppet 'gained entry into the world by a mysterious loophole in its metaphysics'. (p. 265) Vampire-like, she sinks her teeth into his throat, and burns down his little theatre. Carter's punitive intentions are made explicit in her Introduction: the puppeteer willed Lady Purple into being because he wanted so much for her to exist, and 'if she destroys him the very minute she comes to life, then it is his own silly fault for thinking such dreadful things in the first place'. (p. x)

As she developed through the 70s and into the 80s, Angela Carter continued her efforts to find ways of writing about an infinitely greater variety of experience than has been possible heretofore, and to say things for which no language previously existed. It is for her of the greatest importance that women should write fiction *as* women; it is part of the process of 'decolonializing our language and our basic habits of thought'.[10] In this respect her intentions are similar to those of Margaret Drabble, but Carter is much more radical and adventurous in staking out new territory and finding new things to say. She takes ideas and images recklessly from sources of all kinds, saying that she regards the whole of Western culture as a kind of folklore, and conversely folklore as the fiction of the poor, and requiring to be taken seriously. She sees herself as being 'in the demythologizing business', and asserts that myths are products of the human mind designed to make people unfree.[11] She is especially concerned with myths about sexuality, saying in the 'Polemical Preface' to her cultural historical study *The Sadeian Woman* (1979): 'Myth deals in false universals, to dull the pain of particular circumstances. In no area is this more true than in that of relations between the sexes. . . . All the mythic versions of women, from the myth of the redeeming purity of the virgin to that of the healing, reconciling mother, are consolatory nonsenses; and consolatory nonsense seems to me a fair definition of myth anyway'. (pp. 5–7) She maintains that the subjection of women has resulted from a process by which culturally defined variables, only partially derived from the fact of sexual differentiation, have been invalidly translated to the status of universals. In her fiction she proceeds to challenge these false universals with vigour.

So in *The Passion of New Eve*, which she conceived as 'a feminist tract about the social creation of femininity', Carter deploys material from myths of Oedipus, Tiresias, Eve, Lilith, and many more sources. It is an anti-mythic novel which uses the picaresque form to portray the adventures of the hero/ine, on a hectic journey through an America which is in the grip of civil unrest. Beginning with a study of Evelyn's (male) sexual excess in a New York which is a nightmare of chaos, the narrative continues to his castration and re-modelling as 'new Eve' at the hands of the Mother who leads a futuristic matriarchy. Eve then suffers as one of a harem controlled by a crazed polygamous poet. Through these episodes, aspects of sexual dominance and submissiveness are explored in extreme and bizarre manifestations. A major theme is Hollywood's construction of sexual stereotypes, handled with dazzling pungency through the screen idol Tristessa, a Tiresias figure because she is eventually revealed as a transvestite.

10. 'Notes From the Front Line', p. 75.
11. Haffenden, *Novelists in Interview*, p. 92, and 'Notes From the Front Line', p. 71.

Carter's Rewriting of Fairy-Tales. *The Bloody Chamber*

Still pursuing the topic of sexuality, Carter goes on to adopt the medium of the fairy tale re-written, a process which she describes as 'relaxing' into folklore after her anti-mythic novel. She published in 1979 under the title *The Bloody Chamber* a collection of her own versions of some classic fairy stories, and she has commented that she found it easier to deal with what she calls the shifting structures of reality and sexuality by using sets of shifting structures derived from orally transmitted traditional tales, rather than myth. The fairy tale allows her to display her Gothic skills to perfection. The experiences are often extreme, sometimes outlandish and macabre, they offer opportunities to describe both glitter and filth, and she is able to write lovingly and lingeringly of luxury, fear, cruelty, decay and death. The tales are short, and, like her own short stories, provide Carter with a form in which she can achieve powerful effects by concentrating pure experience within a short narrative trajectory.

For a feminist the treatment of fairy tales presents a very obvious challenge, because patriarchal assumptions are so fundamental to their structure. Andrea Dworkin has observed that fairy tales confirm stereotypes in which men and women are absolute opposites: 'The heroic prince can never be confused with Cinderella, or Snow-White, or Sleeping Beauty. She could never do what he does at all, let alone better'.[12] In the traditional fairy tale view, women are either 'good', and to be possessed, or 'bad', and to be destroyed. There are ways in which the traditional values can be subverted, so as to turn them into vehicles for a different ideology. Feminist strategies have included straightforward reversal of the facts of the narrative, as in the Merseyside Fairy Story Collective's new version of Little Red Riding Hood, in which a timid heroine grows brave at the moment of crisis and, with the help of her aged great-grandmother, kills the wolf. Thereafter she goes about spreading courage among other frightened children. An alternative approach is to rewrite the tale ironically, as in Suniti Namjoshi's treatment of the Bluebeard story, in which the returning husband is amazed and incensed to find that his bride has *not* disobeyed him by entering the forbidden room, and kills her on the spot.[13]

Carter favours instead an indirect approach, and so she retains the

---

12. Andrea Dworkin, *Our Blood: Prophecies and Discourses on Sexual Politics* (The Women's Press, 1982), p. 55.
13. Suniti Namjoshi, *Feminist Fables*, (Sheba, 1984).

essential facts of the tales she tells, thus accepting structures that are for the most part dictated by male initiatives. Within these structures she modifies details, changes perspectives, or introduces a different mood. Without moving far from the outlines of the traditional stories, she is able to make the female roles more positive, or sometimes simply to change the story by giving prominence to the female point of view.

The attraction of the fairy tale lies in the far-fetched and the wonderful, and for Carter such material can be used to advance understanding of experience. She finds some of the most fruitful possibilities in the notions about interaction between animal and human worlds, which allow her new ways of exploring aspects of sexuality. Repeatedly she re-works stories of sexual encounters between humans and animals: in two versions of the 'Beauty and the Beast' story she shows women accepting a lion and a tiger as mates.[14] In 'The Company of Wolves' (which has received wider circulation as a film for which Carter collaborated with Neil Jordan in the writing of the screen-play) she produces a remarkably original version of the Red Riding Hood story, in which the girl, instead of being eaten by a cunning and hungry wolf, is confronted by a werewolf figure and takes him as her lover. Jack Zipes, discussing Carter's treatment of the story in *The Trials and Tribulations of Little Red Riding Hood*, points out that in the most popular forms of the story Red Riding Hood is a male creation, and reflects men's fear of women's sexuality by showing the girl to be to blame for her own death, or symbolic rape. Carter, by contrast, shows a strong-minded young woman who can fend for herself and can tame the wolf by the positive use of her sexuality.[15]

Maggie Anwell has observed that there are significant differences between this story and the film based on it.[16] She agrees with Zipes in finding a positive approach to sexuality in the story, and points to significant differences between the story, which asserts female power, and the film version, in which modifications distort the expression of this idea. She emphasizes that Carter's story changes the passive victim of the Perrault version of Little Red Riding Hood into a strong, active protagonist. She finds in her treatment a radical re-telling which

---

14. 'The Courtship of Mr Lyon' and 'The Tiger's Bride', in *The Bloody Chamber*, p. 41 and p. 51.
15. Jack Zipes, *The Trials and Tribulations of Little Red Riding Hood: Versions of the Tale in Sociocultural Context* (Heinemann, 1983), pp. 56–7.
16. Maggie Anwell, 'Lolita Meets the Werewolf: *The Company of Wolves*' in Lorraine Gamman and Margaret Marshment, ed., *The Female Gaze* (The Women's Press, 1988), pp. 76–85.

emphasizes the protagonist's strength, necessary in a savage world, and the power of her virginity which she is willing to discard at the appropriate moment, in a process of successful negotiation which brings the girl to sleep eventually between the paws of the wolf. Anwell finds the film to be inferior because it is unable to handle the image of the girl confident of her own desire for sexual experience in the relation with the animal. It replaces the final image of young woman and wolf with a confusing ending in which she changes into a wolf and the two animals escape together. As Anwell points out, this does not serve the purpose of the story; it is part of an approach which for commercial reasons places a high value on the special effects involved in transformation scenes, and sacrifices imaginative subtlety in return for a deadening sort of literalness. The distinguishing characteristic of Carter's telling of the story, and indeed of her writing generally, is precisely the reverse of deadening literalness.

Issues relating to power and sexuality emerge in a more problematic form in Carter's version of the tale of Bluebeard, 'The Bloody Chamber', to which she gives prominence by making it the title story of the collection. The traditional interaction between the powerful, sadistic husband and his innocent, curious bride is retained, although translated into the settings of rich French twentieth-century life, so that Bluebeard has a deliciously romantic castle in Brittany, provided with a telephone on which he can call his stockbroker. As a piece of Gothic style it is perfect, in its juxtaposition of sharply realized pleasure and pain, and the entry of material from the contemporary world sharpens the sensations through its apparent incongruity. The story is given a new direction by the location of the narrative in the perception of the virgin bride, rather than in the voice of an impersonal third-person narrator. There is a small but significant alteration in the facts of the narrative: the young wife is saved from her husband, not, as in traditional forms of the tale, by her brothers, but surprisingly by her mother who telepathically learns that her daughter is in danger. Thus female consciousness, and the possibility of female power, are admitted into the story.

Although the tale is thus modified, it retains the sexual violence which is one of the essentials of the Bluebeard material, and Carter evokes this in vivid detail. This has disturbed some feminist critics who find in her handling of such material something that comes uncomfortably close to pornography. Patricia Duncker, for example, finds in Carter's exploration of the tensions between female fear and acceptance of the male a version of essentially pornographic material of male domination and possession.[17] Paulina Palmer sees 'The Bloody Chamber' as coming close to pornography in the vividness with which it treats sadistic and masochistic material, but considers that it may be rendered acceptable by the location of the narrative voice in the victim, and by the denouement in which the heroine's mother asserts female power.[18] For both of these critics pornography is an unacceptable manifestation of the humiliation of women and the assertion of male power. However the issues raised by pornography and the erotic are very contentious ones in feminist thinking. There are divisions between those who hold that 'pornography is the theory, rape the practice', and others for whom the logic of their ideas about personal liberty demands that pornography should be not be condemned. Angela Carter herself rejects the simple view that pornography is harmful to women. Her writing about the erotic is shaped by desire for female autonomy, and she is more adventurous in her attitude to artistic expression of the erotic than many of her critics. She has expressed her ideas on pornography in the 'Polemical Preface' to her highly original study of de Sade, *The Sadeian Woman*, which is full of shrewd insights into the relationship between power and sexuality. Following her own radical instincts she sees pornography as potentially liberating for women, and in her study of de Sade she points out that he was unusual in his period in claiming rights of free sexuality for the female. (p. 36) She contemplates the possibility of a 'moral pornography' which would offer a critique of current relations between the sexes, and produce 'a revelation, through the infinite modulations of the sexual act, of the real relations of man and his kind. Such a pornographer would not be the enemy of women, perhaps because he might begin to penetrate to the heart of the contempt for women that distorts our culture even as he enters the realms of true obscenity as he describes it.' (pp. 19–20)

A common feature in the critical approach of Palmer and Duncker lies in distrust of heterosexual assumptions. Duncker's view of Carter is that while her tales are supposedly celebrations of erotic desire, she has not in fact succeeded in developing a language which is sufficiently free from long-established links between male sexuality and power. She finds Carter's psychology of the erotic 'deeply, rigidly sexist',

17. Patricia Duncker, 'Reimagining the Fairy Tales: Angela Carter's Bloody Chambers', in Peter Humm, Paul Stigant and Peter Widdowson, ed., *Popular Fictions* (Methuen, 1986), pp. 222–36.
18. Palmer, 'Coded Mannequin', p. 189.

arguing that she sees women's sensuality simply as a response to male arousal, and has no conception of women's sexuality as autonomous desire'.[19] Duncker clearly feels dissatisfaction with Carter because the novelist does not share her own attitudes, and the terms in which she writes suggest that she sees any female response to male initiatives as incompatible with female autonomy. Her criticism does not do justice to the extent to which Carter explores women's sexual experience. Palmer also values highly fiction which progresses beyond what she sees as the oppressively heterosexist norms that dominated the cultural climate of the 1960s. She therefore approves a difference in emphasis which she detects in Carter's later work. She suggests, persuasively, that although in all Carter's story-telling an analytic and demytho-logizing tendency coexists with a celebratory and utopian one, it is possible to characterize her output up to and including *The Passion of New Eve* as being predominantly concerned to analyse the oppressive effects of patriarchal social structures. Since 1978, she has placed more emphasis on female power and possibilities for change. Palmer finds in *The Bloody Chamber* the beginnings of this woman-centred approach, and a capacity to envisage liberation in personal life and new directions in the organization of society, qualities which are more fully developed in the remarkable eighth novel, *Nights at the Circus*.

Carter's Female Comedy. *Nights at the Circus*

Nights at the Circus resembles *The Passion of New Eve* in being picaresque, and fantastic, and in incorporating analysis of feminist ideas, but it is a far richer and more successful novel. It is a comic work, filled with suspense and wonder, telling the story of a larger-than-life female acrobat who is known familiarly as 'Fevvers' because she has wings. She is an image of female capacity, resourcefulness, and wit. She joins the circus in London, in the closing months of the nineteenth century, and travels with it to Petersburg, where she escapes the rapacious advances of a Grand Duke. The circus proceeds on the transcontinental journey towards Japan, but on the way through Siberia the train is dynamited by outlaws who believe mis-takenly that Fevvers is to marry the Prince of Wales, and wish to hold her hostage, hoping by these means to exert pressure politically on the Tsar. Within this extravagant framework Fevvers functions as a focus

19. Duncker, 'Reimagining the Fairy Tales', pp. 227–28.

for improbabilities and impossibilities of various sorts. She may have been hatched, not born, in parody of the origin of Helen of Troy; she escapes from deadly situations by means that are not specified and that would not be available to a woman with normal powers; she and her foster mother possess a clock which does strange things with time, and a small sword which, until it is broken, provides her with supernatural protection. The marvels extend to animals possessed of powers of feeling and thinking normally attributed only to humans. The Colonel's pig, Sibyl, tells fortunes, and the circus apes, although lacking the powers of speech, have the capacity to negotiate their contract in writing, and eventually to make the decision to catch the train for Helsinki instead of going on to Siberia. The anthropomorphism is pervasive. Even animals whose behaviour remains within normal limits are presented as having emotions like those of humans. The female tiger attacks a human performer, and has to be shot, because she suffers intolerable jealousy at seeing her mate dance with the woman. The narrator is always mindful of the animals' perspective, as when she notes the cloakroom in which furs are left during circus performances, which 'became a treasury of skins of sable, fox and precious little rats, as though there one left behind the skin of one's own beastliness so as not to embarrass the beasts with it'. This play of fancy is anchored firmly in an awareness of the realities of circus life. The action takes place in an aroma of 'horse dung and lion piss', in a world in which the tiger-keeper wears 'a terrible apron stiff with blood from waitressing her carnivores'. (Part 2, Ch. 2, pp. 105–6)

Set within a series of preposterous adventures there is a central comic story focused on Fevvers, the essence of which is in the resourcefulness with which Fevvers repeatedly resists manipulation by male authority figures. This presentation of female power is balanced against the humiliation of the American journalist, Jack Walser, who is so fascinated by Fevvers that he joins the circus and consents to act the role of The Human Chicken. There is a reversal here of the humiliation of females by males which has been a feature of some of Carter's earlier work, and as Carter herself comments, Walser actually consents to his own humiliation.[20] The plot brings the relationship between Fevvers and Walser to a happy conclusion, and the narrative is dominated by the young woman's cheerful zest for life and pleasure in her powers. Both she and Liz, her foster mother, have more than normal insight – Liz is at some points seen as having the characteristics

20. Haffenden, *Novelists in Interview*, p. 92.

of a sibyl – and both possess gifts of fluent and graphic speech, so that ideas of female control and authority are emphasized. The comic treatment of sexual politics dovetails throughout with subplots which portray horrifically the inhumanity of man to woman in, for example, the fearful history of Mignon, whose father killed her mother and drowned himself, and who grew up to be beaten like a carpet by the ape man. This theme is amplified by little Ivan who tries to run away with the circus, whose mother, after too many beatings, killed his father with an axe. Both of these narrative strands are handled so that they inscribe, in different ways, a positive view of female being. Mignon finds happiness in a lesbian relationship with the tiger-keeper, which is established in lyrical fashion when they tune a neglected piano in the Siberian wastes and together perform Mignon's song in a marvellous harmony with tigers that lie on the roof of the house, 'laid low by pleasure', golden and ecstatic. The apparent tragedy of Ivan's mother is transformed, in a utopian solution in which a group of women, kept in a penitentiary because they have murdered their husbands, form a sisterly alliance with their female warders, break out of their prison, and set off to found a new female society in the wilderness. They take with them a supply of frozen sperm with which they hope to ensure the survival of their little republic. The utopian vision is qualified by the irony of Liz's practical response: 'What'll they do with the boy babies? Feed them to the polar bears? To the *female* polar bears?' (Part 3, Ch. 7, pp. 240–1)

This flamboyant and fantastic material is placed in a specific historical context. The narrative is located in the closing months of the nineteenth century, with a new age about to dawn. Revolution is comically introduced through Liz's unexpected political activity: she is secretly taking advantage of Walser's journalistic communications to send reports back to England on the political struggle in Russia, keeping a promise she had made to 'a spry little gent . . . she met in the reading-room of the British Museum'. (Envoi, p. 292) Liz has a sharp political awareness, some of which she has passed on to Fevvers, and best expressed in the acrobat's reaction to the hopelessly naive outlaws who have captured her: 'Nobility of spirit hand in hand with absence of analysis, that's what's always buggered up the working class.' (Part 3, Ch. 5, p. 232) Wider perspectives are introduced, in the conferring of representative qualities on the people of the circus. Managed by an optimistic American, it contains performers from a range of European nationalities, possessing significant characteristics, most prominently Mignon, German by birth, who carries the symbolism of the sorrows of Europe as well as that of abused womanhood. This picture of Western life is set against the culture of primitive societies in the shaman who enters the book in the Siberian section, thus giving the novel a remarkably comprehensive range.

Nights at the Circus is a work of artifice in the currently fashionable mode which, sometimes almost predictably, has authors giving themselves parts in their own fictions and playing games with their readers. Both Fevvers and Liz are used conspicuously and comically as vehicles for things that the author wishes to have said, as when Liz draws attention self-reflexively to the notion that the circus people could be viewed as 'a microcosm of human society . . . an emblematic company' (Part 3, Ch. 10, p. 279), and Victoria Glendinning has suggested that the voice given to Fevvers is at times the voice of 'some earnest student of the works of Angela Carter'.[21] Carter shows an exuberant disregard for convention by mingling narrative voices and using inconsistent time-schemes. There is a baroque quality in the rich proliferation of subsidiary stories which grow both backwards and into the future. Yet the whole fiction is controlled by a central design organized around a series of escapes: Fevvers's own escape from the rapacious Grand Duke, Walser's escapes in the circus from a jealous tiger and a crazed clown, and the escape of the women from their Siberian house of correction. In *Nights at the Circus* Carter has produced a fiction in which pity and horror are treated soberly, and are nevertheless in due course validly incorporated into a joyful comic vision that asserts female strength and intelligence.

Emma Tennant. *The Bad Sister* and *Queen of Stones*

Emma Tennant shares with Angela Carter a vigorous and inventive approach to fiction, and the ability to move with ease between different ways of representing experience. She is innovative, and has a highly developed interest in what is happening beneath the surface of events, which leads her to make extensive use of metaphor and symbol. She adapts myths to her own purposes, and builds fictions on sources from earlier literature. She is progressive and feminist in her thinking, although she comes from a socially privileged background which she sees as being in a sense disadvantageous because, as she says, it makes

21. Review by Victoria Glendinning, *The Sunday Times* 30 September 1984, p. 42.

it difficult for a writer to be taken seriously.[22] She resembles Carter in coming from a family with Scottish origins, and for each of them this provides an external point of reference which may be a source of insight. Although Angela Carter was born and brought up in England, her father was a Scottish journalist who worked in England and eventually retired to live again in North-East Scotland. She says of herself, 'I always felt foreign in England, and I realized the reason I'd always felt foreign was that I was. (My father) never perceived himself as Scottish, as being different, but it *is* different, I think.'[23]

For Emma Tennant the Scottish experience is more tangible – she spent a war-time childhood at Glen House in the Scottish borders, an ancestral home belonging to her father's family. She describes her childhood as 'extremely beautiful and isolated', and the shock of being moved to London after the war was like expulsion from her childhood Eden.[24] Scotland is, for her 'where I happen to come from and where my imagination – it seems to me – is so completely unlike a lot of English novelists'.[25] She is a versatile novelist who has written in contrasting modes: some of her novels are extravagant imaginings of events in an apocalyptic future, some are plotless poetic treatments of mood and consciousness, and in several she has produced a perceptive analysis of aspects of female being in the context of contemporary life.

The Scottish part of her heritage is used productively in her novel *The Bad Sister* (1978), which is based on James Hogg's *The Private Memoirs and Confessions of a Justified Sinner*, a grim nineteenth-century Scottish narrative which deals with demonic possession, and in which a Calvinist convinced of his election to grace has an *alter ego* who commits murder and other terrible crimes. Tennant's interest in Hogg derives partly from the fact that he lived in the part of the Borders where she spent her early childhood – he wrote stories about the wood outside her bedroom window – but she is also deeply interested in his treatment of the idea of the double, a recurrent concern of Gothic writing. Whether or not Scots are more severely affected than other nationalities by the divided self, they believe that they are, and Tennant is well aware of the extent to which this consciousness is manifested in Scottish literature. She takes the Scottish divided self from Hogg's story and transposes it into the late

22. Sue Roe and Emma Tennant, 'Women Talking About Writing' in Moira Monteith, ed., *Women's Writing. A Challenge to Theory* (Harvester Press, 1986), p. 147.
23. Sage, 'The Savage Sideshow', p. 286.
24. Haffenden, *Novelists in Interview*, pp. 282–3.
25. 'Women Talking About Writing', p. 124.

twentieth century, using as her protagonist a young woman appropriately named Jane Wild, through whom she can explore deeply disturbing aspects of dividedness in contemporary female experience. Extreme Calvinism is replaced by an extreme form of radical feminism. Tennant is in general sympathetic to feminism, but she depicts in the novel adherents of a fanatical form of militant feminism, who influence Jane, and who justify the killing of her father as a symbolic assassination of capitalism and paternalism. Hogg's use of the demonic double is the source for Jane's relationship with her 'bad sister', under whose influence she commits murder. Hogg also provides the basic form of the book – a first-person journal written by Jane, enclosed between two pieces of prosaic background material emanating from a fictitious editor who provides an external, rational perspective. The narrative is therefore open to varying interpretations. The editor's conclusion contains a psychiatric diagnosis of schizophrenia, of a trite kind which invites dissent, and the reader is left unsure how Jane is to be understood. Tennant has confirmed in an interview that to see her as a paranoid schizophrenic is too simple. She is interested in pressures exerted on women's identity, and the damaging effects of the necessity to conform to social expectations, which creates a kind of wildness by standing in the way of self-expression. And, pursuing the particular problems of the woman as artist, she draws attention to the idea in the novel that the woman who thinks 'must live with a demented sister', and to the thought, suggested by Virginia Woolf, that a woman writer calls down a female muse who 'gives her a hearty kick on the shin'.[26]

Within Jane's narrative there is a continuous interaction between a sharp portrayal of a mundane reality and the dreams and delusions experienced by Jane. Tennant accomplishes transitions fluently, making use of metaphor to express states of mind, as when in a vision of a beautiful clearing in a shining, metallic forest, Jane attains and then loses contact with a benevolent male figure extraordinarily like herself. (pp. 78–80) Randall Stevenson has observed that a particular strength of *The Bad Sister* is that its juxtaposition of the drab, colourless world and the dimension of dreams is used to develop specific criticisms of the former, and of women's place in it. He points to how Tennant's fantasy is employed to satiric purpose, through Jane's perceptions of current social conventions, as when she sees on advertisement hoardings 'the housewife suspended in the vapours of her pie, her smile

26. 'Women Talking About Writing', p. 125.

moistened in the wreaths of animal fat coming up at her like winter breath'.[27] This is a complex novel, in which Tennant moves easily between surface reality and dark forces of the mind. The combination of psychological insight with a consideration of sexual politics makes it an important document in the exploration of female identity and female creativity.

In *Alice Fell* (1980), Tennant takes another aspect of female being for her subject, and uses myth and allegory to deal with a girl's growing up. Her concern is to follow the stages of development from infancy to Alice's 'fall' in adolescence, and to express a feeling of pessimism about the limited opportunities life offers to girl children. The myth of Persephone, used as a framework, helps to define the idea of the daughter lost, or snatched, or destined to be gone at the end of summer. Retrospectively Tennant has expressed some dissatisfaction with the result, suggesting that the mythic pattern is overschematic. It is inevitably a narrative with a predetermined outcome, as indeed the title makes clear, but the progression through the text to the climax, using recurrent symbols of the seasons and of shapes and colours, produces a novel of great beauty and power.

In her next novel, *Queen of Stones* (1982), Tennant pursues her interest in how society treats women, and particularly young women, and this time concentrates on adolescence and pre-adolescence. Her story is an account of an incident in which a party of adolescent and pre-adolescent girls are lost in fog in Dorset, a number of stresses in the relationships between them are manifested, and eventually one, who is marked by different social class as an outsider, is killed. Two male-authored texts lie behind *Queen of Stones* and are in a sense sources. In part Tennant is producing a female version of William Golding's *Lord of the Flies*, which provides a source for the isolation, the extreme experience, and the emergence of inhumanity among children. The other important text is Freud's account of the case of Dora, his *Fragment of an Analysis of a Case of Hysteria*, which Tennant parodies in her treatment of the male psychiatrist's dealings with one of the young women in her story. Feminists have found much to interest them in this essay of Freud's, which contains fascinating material relating to his assumptions about, among other things, the nature of femininity. Freud's confidence that he knew what was wrong with Dora now looks clearly misguided – as Steven Marcus remarks, he is

27. Randall Stevenson, *The British Novel Since the Thirties. An Introduction* (Batsford, 1986), p. 160. Tennant, *The Bad Sister* (Picador, 1979), p. 38.

'at once dogmatically certain and very uncertain'.[28] Tennant gives her character Bess some of 'Dora's' symptoms, coughing and loss of voice, and she is seen by a psychiatrist who confidently attributes these symptoms, in Freudian style, to her feeling that her father has rejected her, and her unconscious imitation of his lack of potency. Tennant's purpose in portraying the inadequacies of the Freudian view is to produce a study of 'how girls are brought up to think of themselves and their expectations'.[29] She is interested both in how society has moulded them, by the influence of fairy-stories and psychological concepts, and also in how society understands them or fails to understand them. Melanie, the victim, is seen as the Beast of Beauty and the Beast. Hansel and Gretel and Goldilocks and the Three Bears shape the girls' views of themselves and their companions. Something of the contradictory nature of childhood experience is suggested through the conjunction of fairy-tale and legendary material with contemporary brand names for sweets and soft drinks.

The problematic nature of this fiction is reflected in the open-ended and inconclusive form Tennant chooses to use. She presents the material as a dossier of documents – a newspaper story, and reports by a psychiatrist and a social worker, together with a comment from a bishop, and a speculative reconstruction of events, all presented by an author/editor. The story is therefore, like *The Bad Sister*, open to various interpretations, depending on which documents are regarded as reliable. Tennant has given some external guidance about what her thinking was, in a discussion with Sue Roe and Moira Monteith in which she explains her purpose as being to examine myths and/or lies about puberty.[30] She has confirmed that certain of the interpretations of events are not meant to be authoritative. Male authority figures, like the psychiatrist and the bishop, use terminology which is ironized; further, the social worker, although female, is using male language, and by means of this device Tennant expresses a critical view of women who adopt male perspectives and terminology. The gender of the narrator remains unclear, but by speaking of, for example, 'the psychopathology of the developing female being more fully comprehended', s/he betrays an approach which if not male has internalized male attitudes and is therefore inappropriate. (p. 37) *Queen of Stones*

28. Charles Bernheimer and Claire Kahane. ed., *In Dora's Case. Freud – Hysteria – Feminism* (Virago, 1985), p. 78.
29. Haffenden, *Novelists in Interview*, p. 298.
30. 'Women Talking About Writing', p. 142.

has a dissolving, elusive quality which represents the difficulty of understanding a situation in which the participants themselves have only a fragmented awareness. In this novel Tennant's imagination and inventiveness produce a very fine analysis of female pre-adolescence.

Sara Maitland. *Virgin Territory*

Sara Maitland identifies herself as both a Christian and a feminist. Daughter of a Scottish family, but educated at an English school and at Oxford, she came in her twenties to Anglo-Catholicism, and she is married to an Anglican clergyman who works in East London. She differs from the many feminists who distrust Christianity as being essentially rooted in patriarchy and inimical to all that they stand for. She has applied herself to the search for a synthesis between her feminism and her Christian faith, and she has commented that this process is not yet so far advanced in Britain as it is in the United States. Maitland believes that there is something lacking in a women's movement which denies the spiritual dimension, and she has worked in this area with other women who share her interests, not all of them Christian and not all practising religion in conventional ways.[31] She is emphatic that religion should not be a kind of shelter from the real world, and her approach to Christianity is political in that she finds in it 'a fundamental leaning towards justice and equality'.[32] Writing in 1988 about her beginnings as a writer of fiction, she explains that when she first became interested in religion, 16 years earlier, she found that there were not 'any books at all that celebrated both the delight and the complexity of spirituality out of the consciousness of feminism'. Her own novels *Daughter of Jerusalem* and *Virgin Territory* were attempts to write what she was looking for. Maitland continues, ' "Not for heterosexual atheists", wrote one reviewer, and for the first time I felt amused compassion. Poor things, I thought. What on earth do they think homosexual deists have been reading at any time during these last one hundred years'.[33] Since then, as she says, her 'smoke signals' have been answered all across the prairie. She cites the English writers Michelene Wandor and Jeanette Winterson, and the American Roman Catholic novelist Mary Gordon, as women who are producing what she admires as serious and joyful writing.

31. Jo Garcia and Sara Maitland, ed., *Walking on the Water* (Virago, 1983), Introduction, pp. 1–5.
32. *The Guardian* 21 September 1983, p. 18.
33. *The Sunday Times* 17 July 1988, p. G 4.

Maitland's account of the difficulties she faced as she developed as a feminist writer has been mentioned in Chapter 3. She found her subject in feminist transformations of old stories, but faced difficulties, over-come with the help of the Feminist Writers' Group, in navigating a way between the aesthetic objection that the imagination will not be held captive to a theory, and the political objection that what she was writing was not sufficiently accessible to most women. In terms of the feminist writer's quest she describes herself as coming through on to a plain where she lived productively for a few years before encountering a fresh difficulty, that 'women choose madness and badness daily' and the feminist writer had to tell these stories as well as the comforting ones, so that she frightened herself with the awareness of the dark side of female nature. She sees herself as having been rescued from this by the existence of her baby daughter, and later also her son. For her the pratical demands of children are not so much a distraction from imaginative life as an anchor in practical reality which gives psycho-logical protection.

Maitland sees her own most congenial form as being the short story, and she has written short stories both in collaboration with the other members of the Feminist Writers' Group, in *Tales I Tell My Mother* (1978) and in her own collection, *A Book of Spells* (1987). But she has also done very distinguished work as a novelist, breaking new ground, making use of metaphor, myth and symbol to explore women's experience of the spiritual as well as of life in more everyday terms. She presents herself as having little enthusiasm for social realism, but as being 'quite interested in muddling around the categories' as in magic realism, and also in reclaiming myths.[34] In her two novels she uses symbols and mythologies boldly in thoroughly contemporary treat-ments of disturbing material. She explains something of her approach to writing fiction, her interests, and her literary preferences, in a comic epistolary fiction she produced together with Michelene Wandor, with the punning title *Arky Types* (1987). This work deals with their plans for collaborating on a book which might treat the subject of Mrs Noah; that book is never written, but in exchanging letters about the projected enterprise Wandor and Maitland elaborate on their ideas about litera-ture, women, and their respective religious heritages. Maitland pin-points what is for her an important feature of her treatment of symbolic figures that proceeds from her Christian belief. As they debate the possibility of writing a book based on a pair of mythical figures,

34. Sara Maitland and Michelene Wandor, *Arky Types* (Methuen, 1987), p. 71.

Maitland explains to Wandor that while for Wandor, Jewish but not religious, Eve is a myth, for herself as a Christian Mary Magdalene is 'not a myth but a sister'. (p. 72) This does not prevent her from adding symbolic significance to New Testament figures, any more than it prevented medieval Christians from creating allegorical meanings for biblical persons. But her position distinguishes her sharply from Carter and Tennant, in that although she shares their interest in exploring symbolic modes of expression, and in subverting patriarchal authority, they are dealing in what they see purely as metaphor, whereas for her there is an underlying reality in some of the terms she employs. Although in some of her work she mixes real figures with invented ones from classical myth, like Persephone, she is always mindful of their different status.

Maitland's first novel, *Daughter of Jerusalem* (1978), deals with the problem of infertility. The traditional figures of barrenness, like the biblical Sarah and Elizabeth, are brought into the context of the modern fertility clinic, and the infertile woman attends the clinic wearing a T-shirt that announces 'I am a humourless feminist'. While longing to be pregnant she still demonstrates in support of women's right to choose not to have a child. Maitland dares to make a connection between menstrual blood and the blood of the Lamb. She brings together deftly the heterogeneous elements of modern women's experience.

Virgin Territory, which followed in 1984, is a bold exploration of tensions generated for a contemporary woman by traditional Christian ideas of virginity, obedience, sexuality and mothering. The ideas are focused through the story of an American nun, Anna, who after the rape of one of her sisters in a Latin American convent, becomes disturbed and travels to London to undertake research and examine her feelings about her vocation. It is a thoroughly unfashionable subject for a feminist. Maitland defies expectations again by introducing into her analysis of Anna a lesbian attraction to a radical feminist whom she meets during her stay in London. Through Anna's interaction with Karen, and the conversations they have, Maitland develops thoughts about misogyny in the church, about masochistic elements in female sexuality and spirituality, and about patriarchal power and the possibility of challenging it.

The novel has a core of narrative similar to the reflection of experience normally found in realist fiction, but the scope and significance of the text are enormously extended by the use of a network of symbols derived from many different sources. The analysis of relations between a woman and the Catholic church is built on a complex system of metaphor. A literal situation in which Anna lacks a mother, and is the youngest of five daughters of a father who values her submissiveness, and her father takes pleasure in handing her over to the Mother Superior, becomes the basis of an extensive exploration of symbolic relationships. In Anna's consciousness the church is dominated by the harsh Fathers, who demand discipline and obedience. There are mothers too, the Mother Superior, Mother Church, Holy Mary Mother of God, but 'all of them very wedded mothers, mothers who were on the side of the Fathers, not on the side of the children'. (Ch. 2, p. 35) In the course of the narrative Anna's need for mothering is revealed, partly through her identification with a handicapped child, Caro, whom she tries to help by working on a programme of daily exercises for her, and partly in the progress of her emotional relationship with Karen, her lesbian feminist friend. Interwoven with the basic symbolism of family relationships there are further ideas about maleness and about virginity which extend the significance of the novel. The traditional symbolism of love between the virgin and the unicorn Christ is present. In addition, the male aggression in the teaching of the religious fathers is connected with difficult material about the past association of the church in South America with killing, rape and robbery, in symbolism which balances the notion of eldorado against that of the virgin forest. Virginity is a key concept, as the title *Virgin Territory* indicates. Maitland explores a positive notion of virginity, as in the virgin forest which is not barren, but is 'virgin because it is unexploited, not in man's control'. (Ch. 1, p. 23) A further level of classical myth associates Anna in patriarchy with Athene, the virgin born by the will of the Father; and Persephone, the stolen daughter, connects Anna, who needs mothering, with the child Caro.

The book is rich and subtle, and too serious and truthful to come to simple conclusions. But such conclusion as can emerge is given powerful expression in terms of the family metaphors. The 'answer' is in a female approach, variously manifested. Anna reads in a book by a Benedictine nun the saying of Pope John Paul I that 'God is Father. Even more, God is mother'. (Ch. 7, p. 230) This crystallizes her awareness of female power, previously imaged in the Visitation of the Virgin Mary to her cousin Elizabeth, and in ideas about a society of powerful Amazon women, derived from material on sixteenth-century exploration. She leaves her order and goes back to South America to 'seek the country of the Mothers', hoping to find her own identity and emotional maturity.

The epigraph to the book, taken from Sheila Rowbotham's collection of feminist writings *Dreams and Dilemmas*, indicates an interest in women's thinking about archetypes: 'For feminists the existence of universal and ahistoric patterns clearly has to be contested because these inevitably confirm and legitimate male power.'[35] This focuses attention on a crucial disagreement within the narrative, between Anna, who believes in the possibility of a universal, transhistorical symbolic patterning in the human mind, and Karen, who argues that mythologies are born out of specific local ideologies and needs, rather in the way that Angela Carter regards myths as 'indulgent consolations'. Karen's analysis of the existing archetypes of women draws on ideas developed by Maitland's friend and fellow feminist writer, Michèle Roberts. In her contribution, 'The Woman Who Wanted to Be a Hero', to the anthology of feminist material on spirituality which Jo Garcia and Maitland edited, Roberts writes of discovering four archetypes which exist within the female psyche: the virgin, the mother, the companion to men, and the sibyl. She had felt that these archetypes were at war within her, but she learned to see them as interconnected, and this system of imagery helped her eventually to see 'that sexuality and spirituality can be connected, need not be at war'. She also comments that the category of the virgin can accommodate the lesbian/ independent woman who is sexual, free and maternal.[36] In *Virgin Territory* Maitland develops this idea about archetypes, through her character Karen, who argues that archetypes of women are created by men to satisfy their own desires and protect them from their inadequacies. The wife and mother, the sex symbol, the friend and companion, and the virgin, she says, form the sides of a square with men in the middle, defining, and keeping it in focus. Karen would wish to add to this analysis that what is missing from the square, from the archetypes, from all the myths, is the lesbian: 'The dyke is the positive image of the negative virgin'. (Ch. 5, p. 132) Although Anna rejects lesbian love, frontiers of thought are advanced when Karen's insight is grafted on to the traditional Christian pattern of the virgin. This vision of female strength is defined when Anna gives Karen a present of a print of the Visitation, 'two strong women leaning on each other's arms', and Karen pronounces that 'the Visitation is the ultimate Dyke moment . . . when two women get together and in love proclaim their freedom, they sing that the personal is the political and from their love will come freedom for all the world'. (Ch. 6, p. 168)

35. Sheila Rowbotham, *Dreams and Dilemmas* (Virago, 1983).
36. 'The Woman Who Wanted to Be a Hero', in *Walking on the Water*, p. 62.

In *Virgin Territory* Maitland demonstrates that religious commitment need not be a straitjacket, and can indeed provide a standpoint
from which most penetrating observations can be made. Michelene
Wandor has commented very perceptively on Maitland's strength as a
writer that she is 'a marvellous and scholarly stylist who dives into
dangerous waters and chooses disturbing content. . . . I think it is the
tension between her knowledge of (dare I say it) hell and the security of
her cultural heritage that provides the tensions and excitements of her
writing.'[37] She writes with conspicuous intelligence, and constructs her
narratives skilfully so that they accommodate density of thought
without becoming excessively abstract. Her fiction ventures boldly
and joyfully into new territories.

Alice Thomas Ellis. *The Sin Eater* and *The Birds of the Air*

Alice Thomas Ellis shares a Christian faith with Sara Maitland, but her
outlook is in most respects quite different. Whereas Maitland combines Christianity with feminism, and therefore is anxious to revise,
and to put into Christian thinking an awareness of women and their
experience, Ellis is stoutly traditional in religion and also explicitly
critical of feminism. She has said that she wrote her first novel as a
reaction against the feminism of the mid-70s, 'because I was fed up
with feminist whining and whingeing. I'm afraid there's no other word
for it. I felt women did themselves no service by adopting such a Poor
Me position. It seemed to me a travesty of womanhood. I wanted to
show a woman who is very powerful, like so many of the women I
know.'[38] The result of this impulse was *The Sin Eater* (1977), and since
then six more novels have followed.

Large parts of Ellis's narratives are composed of material which
could be accommodated in realist fiction, but they are rendered more
colourful than is normal for realist writing by an element of
exaggeration in her treatment of character, and a taste for the bizarre.
She has a strong sense of the supernatural, partly in consequence of her
acceptance of Christianity of a traditional sort, but she goes beyond
the requirements of Christian orthodoxy in being eager to consider
that, as she puts it, 'There are more things in heaven and earth . . .'
than can be accounted for by material explanation.[39] Some of her

37. *Arky Types*, p. 170.
38. Valerie Grove, *The Compleat Woman* (Chatto & Windus, 1987), p. 237.
39. *Bookmark*, BBC TV, December 1987.

novels include the possibility of ghost or miracle or some other supernatural process. These are introduced disconcertingly into the everyday world, as in *The 27th Kingdom* (1982), which is in part an authentic reconstruction of life in Chelsea in the 50s, including appropriate topical references to homosexual spies and the hanging of Ruth Ellis for killing her lover, but which also contains as major characters a young West Indian nun, Valentine, who is able to perform miracles, and Aunt Irina, the sister of the Abbess Berthe, who 'truly possessed a psychic gift and was not a liar'. (Ch. 2, p. 34) In those books which do not contain supernatural events, God and the saints are familiarly present in the minds of some of the characters, as for example in *The Birds of the Air* (1980), in which Mary Marsh, grieving over the death of her son Robin, and resigned rather than enthusiastic in her religious belief, reflects on God's intentions towards her: 'She saw no reason to suppose that he meant her well in the accepted meaning of that term. . . . She sometimes thought he might have left her Robin, but that wasn't his way.' (p. 85) Ellis's novels are slender, densely packed, and brisk, and her vision frequently combines the comic with the macabre – all features which place her in a line of descent from Muriel Spark.

In some of her novels Ellis uses methods of narration which emphasize the limitation of the characters' perceptions or understanding. In *The Sin Eater* the story is told largely through the consciousnesses of two characters, Rose and Ermyn, who see things but are not always able to interpret them, so that they both fail to grasp the significance of a sinister sexual relationship between Michael and Gomer which has serious consequences. The narrator knows that Ermyn is slightly deaf, although no-one in the story, not even Ermyn herself, is aware of this. Sometimes an omniscient narrative voice draws attention to itself, as at the point where the action of *The 27th Kingdom* ends, and the story-teller mentions that she (or he) was in a pub by the river Thames at the time, without considering it necessary to explain how she comes to know the thoughts that the Reverend Mother was having at that moment in Wales. In this novel omniscience extends to semi-serious reporting of the thoughts of Aunt Irina's cat, indicating the width of perspective at which the fiction aims, e.g. 'Focus had been made a eunuch for the sake of the sweetness of the air in Dancing Master House. He was glad, because it enabled him to take a removed and measured view of affairs – human, feline and, indeed, divine'. (Ch. 3, p. 111) In *Unexplained Laughter* Ellis uses, alongside a conventional third-person narrator, an additional narration in the voice of Angharad, the mentally handicapped child. Angharad cannot speak, and the adulterous lovers she observes believe her incapable of understanding, but she addresses the reader, in typographically distinct passages, sometimes poetically contemplating light and darkness, or death, or the calling of the owls, but more often reporting crisply what the lovers have said or done, or even predicting what they are about to do. These procedures, in suggesting the limitations of human understanding, have an affinity with Muriel Spark's use of omniscience, in which the fact that only the narrator knows all in the fiction reflects the fact that in reality only God knows everything.

In Ellis's novels themes are expressed through traditional Christian symbolism, interwoven with networks of imagery, and often blended with a rich fabric of reference from legend or fairytale. *The Sin Eater* is dominated by death, being constructed around the imminent death of the Captain, the master of Plas Elys, but containing also repeated references to road accidents, and moving towards the hint of a deliberately contrived accident, involving the wrong victims, at the end of the narrative. Ermyn, the daughter of the dying man, through whose consciousness much of the story is told, sees images of death wherever she looks, recalling as she walks on the mountain a seagull impaled on a lightning conductor, a tale of a gamekeeper's suicide, and the legendary death of a Welsh prince. There is a related focus on sin, which Ellis creates by engineering a clash between the ancient Welsh tradition of the 'cup of death', in which at a funeral food or drink is consumed in order to relieve the corpse of its sins, and the doctrine that it is the blood of the lamb that takes away the sins of the world. The legend of the Welsh saint, who has imprinted her being on the North Welsh landscape of the novel, contributes its harshness to the atmosphere of the book. She was an 'angry girl . . . given to lecturing her father and his court on his profligate ways', who showed no concern when their court was inundated by the sea, but retreated to high ground in search of lonely sanctity. (pp. 76–7) This princess-saint has caused the death of the legendary prince, in retribution for his having eaten her pet lamb, and legend also tells that the lamb takes on flesh and wool and life every spring in a symbol of Resurrection. There is a similar interweaving of Christian symbol with legend and folklore in *The Birds of the Air*, giving expression to the magnitude and universality of grief and also placing them in a context of a religion which incorporates recognition of suffering into itself. The central character, Mary, is consumed with grief over the accidental death of her son, Robin, and images and symbols from several sources connect in her mind. The birds of the air, as in the nursery rhyme, should mourn for Robin, although for Mary herself weeping is insufficient and inappropriate. Thinking at Christmas time about her dead son's bones clasped in an ice-bound grave, Mary remembers the old custom of the pursuit and killing of the wren on the day after Christmas, 'such a sad, angry, Godless day', and carrying the dead caged bird around the village before burying it in the churchyard to allay misfortune for the coming year. She also calls to mind a strange old Welsh story in which the dead birds from the Christmas feast are restored to life by a holy man – 'a reversal of the Law, a kind of resurrection, irritating alike to the hungry and the rational'. (p. 89) She resolves that she does not wish to celebrate Christmas: she will wait for the 'godly legerdemain' of Easter. 'Resurrection, after all, was the *pièce de résistance*, deserving only of the roll of drums, the fanfare, the held breath'. (p. 78)

The first powerful woman Ellis created is Rose in *The Sin Eater*. Her interest in power is selective, as she indicates by referring with disapproval to 'women wanting to be like men', but within the limits of traditional female roles she shows female characters who are strong-minded, clever, and competent.[40] Aunt Irina is made to reflect on one unquestionably significant area of power: 'When you thought of the power wielded by the cook, it was tantamount to taunting the driver on a hairpin bend. Even for cooks without access to datura or chopped-up panthers' whiskers there were umpteen varieties of dubious fungi – to some of which there was absolutely no antidote.' (Ch. 3, p. 104) Cooking is for Rose a major area in which she can exercise power. As she practises it, it is neither menial nor repetitive. It is an art, it is theatrical, and it offers her opportunities for malice and practical jokes, as when she cooks a disablingly rich meal for the participants before the annual cricket match is played against the summer visitors.

Rose comes from a different background from the rest of the family she has married into, and through her relations with the others Ellis produces an analysis of cultural and religious difference. Rose is from a Catholic family with Irish roots, and she has the confidence to look at her family by marriage from the viewpoint of an outsider and to know that her taste and views are preferable to theirs. She is contemptuous in particular of her English sister-in-law, Angela, who is vulgarly obsessed by matters of social caste, while Rose knows that such things do not matter and delights in violating social taboos. In religion she

40. *Bookmark*, BBC TV, December 1987.

values traditional truths and ritual beauty. She is scathing about the modernized liturgy, and about Catholic services at which they sing 'Shall we gather at the river', and her stance is contrasted with the vapid religious attitudes adopted by the Anglican bishop and his wife. Sensible religion is a contradiction in terms, she says, her essential position being that she stands where she has always stood, while the church has ebbed away. Ellis, like Muriel Spark, creates characters who have an awareness of death, judgement, heaven, and hell. It is said of the dead Joanna in Spark's *The Girls of Slender Means* that she had a 'sense of hell', and Valentine in *The 27th Kingdom* has a similar consciousness of good and evil, of death and hell and heaven.

In Rose, as also in Mary in *The Birds of the Air*, Ellis shows a woman in whom tough-mindedness is combined with the vulnerability of maternal feeling. Rose is devoted to her five-year-old twins, whose safety is threatened by a combination of accident and misunderstanding and the quasi-maternal passion another woman feels for her grandson. The dreadful threat to their peace of mind that women incur by loving is a recurrent theme in Ellis's work. Her fullest expression of the complexity of motherhood is found, despite the fragmented way in which it is articulated, in Mary in *The Birds of the Air*. At times she comes close to a complete statement of the pain of life, given added force by bitter puns: 'It seemed hard that mothers should be the means of letting into the trap that was life those creatures they loved best in the world. For despite their designation the entrance was not entrancing, not the exit exciting. And the space between held more of bitterness than was promised with the salt, the balm, the joyous clear water and the white cloth of baptism.' (pp. 43–4)

Angela Carter is one of the most vigorously imaginative novelists working in English today. Although she often makes use of established forms, such as the fairy-tale and the picaresque, she is exuberantly inventive in adapting them to accommodate new insights and new ways of looking at familiar material. She reclaims old stories and mythologies to produce fiction which is at the same time satisfying in its concreteness and conceptually strong. Emma Tennant has a similarly innovative approach, adapting and mingling genres to suit her own purposes, and by these means achieving an acute and often very subtle scrutiny of contemporary life. Carter and Tennant are both adept in handling metaphor and symbol, and in manipulating transitions between different levels of experience. They share with Sara Maitland a capacity to use traditional culture as a basis from which to go forward boldly to uncover new perceptions, and to produce a world of the imagination in which female experience receives a just valuation. All three of these novelists revel in the freedom to go beyond realism, which enables them to question and challenge familiar ways of seeing, and to create new possibilities. Male authors also take advantage of such freedoms, but for women, who have more reason to wish to be subversive, the opportunities offered by dreams, fantasies, dissolving structures, and extended metaphors are especially significant. By contrast, Alice Thomas Ellis is distinctive among women writing today in the extent to which, even more than Anita Brookner, she adheres to a traditional ordering of priorities. She is consciously, even defiantly, out of step with much contemporary thinking. It is nevertheless important to note and do justice to her achievement. She is brilliantly successful in developing a kind of fiction in which old certainties can be placed in the context of contemporary conditions.

Conclusion

Although the novelists considered in this study constitute a group in the sense that most of them were born in the 1930s or 1940s, and their careers have developed over the same quarter-century since the early 1960s, they are essentially ten individuals, not unified in outlook or attitude. Their responses to life in the latter part of the twentieth century display some similarities, but the differences between them are at least as interesting. By virtue of being female they have some shared experience, but their lives and their imaginations are in many ways quite separate. They produce analyses of society as varied as those of Pat Barker and Margaret Drabble, and they incorporate into their fiction ideas as different as those of A.S. Byatt and Alice Thomas Ellis.

Not all women novelists wish to give priority to women's affairs. But for the majority of the women discussed in this book, consciousness of gender becomes part of their material, although it is manifested in a spectrum of responses from Ellis's defence of traditional female roles to Angela Carter's tough questioning of received ideas. Pure feminist propaganda does not appeal to any of the writers I have discussed. Both Carter and Drabble are specifically critical of Marilyn French's *The Women's Room*, which is a competent example of polemical feminist fiction, and indicate that they wish to see life in a more complex way than French does. Of the ten novelists, Sara Maitland and Zoe Fairbairns are the most consciously political about their feminism, but they choose to express it in imaginative ways, creating fictional worlds within which attention can be paid to ideas about the female half of human experience. Pat Barker's fiction, and much of Fay Weldon's, are written with a special commitment to making good the neglect or over-simplification that woman as subject has tended to suffer in the past. Other writers, like Drabble, prefer to use a wider focus, but to put female experience and values in a prominent position in their imagined worlds. Generally, women write today with greater confidence that a woman's life is as interesting as a man's. Indeed, since women's expression has been in the past more confined by modesty, and their books have often had limited circulation, there is more opportunity for them to say things that are not already familiar. What Elaine Showalter has called the 'wild zone' is there for novelists to develop, as for instance Weldon does in her direct and vigorous treatment of sexuality, and Maitland in her engagement with issues that arise out of sisterhood and lesbian love. The impetus to look more closely into female experience has stimulated, in particular, more complex and interesting fictional treatments of mothering.As well as fresh and concrete presentations of the physical experiences of maternity, and new versions of the old subject of maternal love, there is also an awareness of the need of the grown woman for mothering, and of the search for 'mothers' beyond the simple biological relationship. Female views are not limited to the personal and the emotional, but extend also into the philosophical, the aesthetic, the cultural and the spiritual. The creative energies of contemporary English women novelists produce work that explores vast tracts of human experience, and is marked by a rich diversity of approach.

Selective Bibliography

Note: Many other relevant works are cited in footnotes to the text. In the case of works published in London the place of publication is omitted.

1 Contemporary Women Novelists

Contemporary Novelists, ed. D.L. Kirkpatrick (St James Press, fourth edition, 1986), contains biographies and brief critical accounts of the work of all the novelists discussed here except for Pat Barker and Sara Maitland. Several are also treated in Randall Stevenson's *The British Novel since the Thirties. An Introduction* (Batsford, 1988), which is of necessity limited in the scale of its treatment of individual authors, but is up-to-date, comprehensive, and reliable. *The Female Form* by Rosalind Miles (Routledge & Kegan Paul, 1987) is a broadly-focused study which examines the female tradition in the novel and its impact on the work of women writing today. Olga Kenyon's *Women Novelists Today. A Survey of English Writing in the Seventies and Eighties* (Brighton, Harvester Press, 1988) devotes a chapter each to Iris Murdoch, A.S. Byatt, Margaret Drabble, Fay Weldon, Eva Figes, and Anita Brookner. *Twentieth-Century Women Novelists*, ed. Thomas F. Staley, (Macmillan, 1982) a miscellaneous collection of essays on writing of the 1960s and 1970s, includes contributions on Murdoch, Drabble, Doris Lessing, and Muriel Spark. Paulina Palmer's *Contemporary Women's Fiction* (Brighton, Harvester Press, 1989) has made a major contribution to the understanding of contemporary women's writing and its relation to literary and feminist theory. Lorna Sage's essay 'Female Fictions: The Women Novelists' in *The Contemporary English Novel*, ed. Malcolm Bradbury and David Palmer (Stratford-Upon-Avon Studies 18, Edward Arnold, 1979), deals briefly but stimulatingly with Murdoch, Drabble, Spark, Lessing, and Angela Carter.

2 Feminism

Hester Eisenstein's *Contemporary Feminist Thought* (George Allen & Unwin, 1984), although it concentrates on American feminism, is an admirably clear, concise guide to the progress of feminist thinking as it has affected British culture also. Mary Evans, ed., *The Woman Question. Readings on the Subordination of Women* (Fontana Paperbacks, 1982) is an extremely valuable source book for feminist thinking, containing about forty key texts or extracts by writers from Mary Wollstonecraft onwards. Betty Friedan's *The Feminine Mystique* (Penguin 1965, first published 1963), although overtaken by more recent thinking, is of historical importance. Juliet Mitchell's title-essay in *Women. The Longest Revolution* (Virago, 1984), which was first published in *New Left Review* 1966, is an important feminist document from a time before the British women's movement existed, and Germaine Greer's *The Female Eunuch* (MacGibbon & Kee, 1970) gave popular currency to many feminist ideas. French feminist thinking is made available in English translations in *New French Feminisms. An Anthology*, edited and introduced by Elaine Marks and Isabelle de Courtivron (Brighton, Harvester Press, 1981), and in Toril Moi, ed., *French Feminist Thought: A Reader* (Oxford, Blackwell, 1987).

Among studies of changes affecting women's lives in Britain, two are particularly valuable. April Carter's *The Politics of Women's Rights* (Longman, 1988) focuses on women's legal rights, their position at work, and their access to political power, in the period since 1945, and assesses the reasons for the changes that have taken place. *Sweet Freedom*, by Anna Coote and Beatrix Campbell (Oxford, Blackwell, new updated edition 1987, first published 1982) gives a full account of the situation of women in Britain, and the effects of the women's movement, since the late 1960s.

3 Women/Feminism and Literature

Comprehensive information on the very large amount of material that now exists on feminist criticism and feminist literary theory is made available by Laura Sue Fuderer in 'Feminist Critical Theory: A Checklist', in *Modern Fiction Studies* 34 (1988), pp. 501–513. This deals with work done between 1973 and 1987. *Making a Difference: Feminist Literary Criticism*, ed. Gayle Greene and Coppelia Kahn (Methuen, New Accents, 1985) provides a range of essays dealing with major aspects of feminist thinking about literature. A very comprehensive survey of the subject is to be found in *Feminist Criticism. Women as Contemporary Critics* by Maggie Humm (Brighton, Harvester Press, 1986). Mary Eagleton's *Feminist Literary Theory. A Reader* (Oxford, Blackwell, 1986) offers a large selection of rather short extracts from works dealing with feminism and literature, usefully arranged in five sections with introductions by Eagleton, relating to different aspects of feminist literary theory. Feminist criticism is discussed by K.K. Ruthven in *Feminist Literary Studies. An Introduction* (Cambridge University Press, 1984) and, much more positively, by Toril Moi in *Sexual/Textual Politics* (Methuen, New Accents, 1985). Moi distinguishes between American and French approaches to feminist literary theory, and her examination of both is illuminating.

Several books address critical problems by way of text-based essays. Mary Jacobus's *Women Writing and Writing About Women* (Croom Helm, 1979) is a collection of essays by several authors on subjects which relate either to how women write or to how they are represented in literature. *Women's Writing. A Challenge to Theory*, ed. Moira Monteith (Brighton, Harvester Press, 1986), makes use of a similar approach, and is organized around ideas about connections between feminist criticism and creative writing. *Women Reading Women's Writing*, ed. Sue Roe (Brighton, Harvester Press, 1987), focuses attention, as the title suggests, on how women read: it contains essays on a range of nineteenth- and twentieth-century writers.

4 Individual Authors

The amount of criticism available on writers dealt with in this book varies enormously. Whereas a bibliography published in 1985 listed more than 130 items dealing with work by Drabble, many of the other novelists discussed here have received little or no critical notice. The following items are of interest:

Angela Carter

'The Savage Sideshow: A Profile of Angela Carter', is a profile and interview by Lorna Sage, first printed in *The New Review* July 1977, and also available in *The New Review Anthology*, ed. Ian Hamilton (Paladin Grafton Books, 1987, first published Heinemann, 1985), pp. 280–299. David Punter includes consideration of *The Passion of New Eve* in *The Hidden Script. Writing and the Unconscious* (Routledge & Kegan Paul, 1985).

Margaret Drabble

A comprehensive listing of the large amount of work done on Drabble up to 1985 is contained in Joan S. Korenman's 'A Margaret Drabble Bibliography', in *Critical Essays on Margaret Drabble*, ed. Ellen Cronan Rose (Boston, Mass., G.K. Hall, 1985).

Margaret Drabble has given many interviews over the years. In addition to those cited in footnotes, the following are particularly interesting: Barbara Milton, 'Margaret Drabble: The Art of Fiction LXX', *The Paris Review* 74 (1978) pp. 40–65; Dee Preussner, 'Talking with Margaret Drabble', *Modern Fiction Studies* 25 (1980), pp. 563–577; and Joanne V. Creighton, 'An Interview with Margaret Drabble', in *Margaret Drabble: Golden Realms*, ed. Dorey Schmidt (Edinburg, Texas, Pan American University School of Humanities, 1982), pp. 18–31.

There are several book-length studies of Drabble. Valerie Grosvenor Myer's *Margaret Drabble: Puritanism and Permissiveness* (Vision Press, 1974) is an early book which offers interesting insights into the novels that come within its scope. Ellen Cronan Rose in *The Novels of Margaret Drabble: Equivocal Figures* (Macmillan, 1980) writes in a dogmatically feminist way, frankly employing adherence to feminist principles as a major criterion in determining value in fiction. She is nevertheless sometimes very shrewd in her analysis of Drabble's texts. Joanne Creighton's *Margaret Drabble* (Methuen, 1985) is the best critical book, offering a concise and consistently very perceptive discussion of Drabble's work. There are also general studies by Mary Hurley Moran: *Margaret Drabble: Existing Within Structures* (Carbondale, Illinois, Southern Illinois University Press, 1983) and by Lynn Veach Sadler: *Margaret Drabble* (Macmillan, 1986).

There are two collections of critical essays, both mentioned above: *Margaret Drabble: Golden Realms* ed. Dorey Schmidt, and *Critical Essays on Margaret Drabble*, ed. Ellen Cronan Rose.

The dominant concerns of articles on Drabble are feminism, and issues relating to developments of realism or to narrative strategies. Marion Vlastos Libby, in 'Fate and Feminism in the Novels of Margaret Drabble', *Contemporary Literature* 16 (1975), pp. 175–192, is concerned with the extent to which Drabble can be described as feminist. Drabble's development of the possibilities of realism is analysed and defended in Michael F. Harper, 'Margaret Drabble and the Resurrection of the English Novel', *Contemporary Literature* 23 (1982) pp. 145–168. Her approach to fiction is also usefully explored in 'Drabble's *The Middle Ground*: "Mid-Life" Narrative Strategies', *Critique* 23 (1982), pp. 69–81, by Ellen Cronan Rose, and in 'The Search for Meaning in Drabble's *The Middle Ground*', *Critique* 23 (1982), pp. 83–93, by Lynn Veach Sadler.

Zoe Fairbairns

Fairbairns's use of the historical saga form is discussed by Lyn Pykett in 'The century's daughters: recent women's fiction and history', *Critical Quarterly* 29 (1987), pp. 71–7.

Biographical Information

Pat Barker

Pat Barker was born in Thornaby-on-Tees in 1943. She was educated at a local grammar school and then studied economics, politics and history at the London School of Economics. She taught at a college of further education in north-east England until the birth of her first child in 1970. She is married to a zoologist, and has a son and a daughter. Pat Barker's novels are *Union Street* (1982, winner of the Fawcett Society Award in 1983), *Blow Your House Down* (1984), *The Century's Daughter* (1986), and *The Man Who Wasn't There* (1989), all published by Virago.

Anita Brookner

Anita Brookner was born in London on 16 July 1928. She was educated at James Allen's Girls' School, Dulwich, and then studied at King's College, University of London, and at the Courtauld Institute of Art. She lectured in history of art at the University of Reading from 1959 to 1964, and from 1964 was lecturer and later reader at the Courtauld Institute. She is an authority on French painting, and her publications include *Watteau* (Hamlyn, 1971), *The Genius of the Future: Studies in French Art Criticism* (Phaidon, 1971), *Greuze: The Rise and Fall of an Eighteenth-Century Phenomenon* (Elek, 1972), and *Jacques-Louis David* (Chatto and Windus, 1980). In 1967–8 she was the first woman to hold the post of Slade Professor at Cambridge. Anita Brookner's novels, all published by Cape, are *A Start in Life*

(1981), *Providence* (1982), *Look at Me* (1983), *Hotel du Lac* (1984, awarded the Booker Prize), *Family and Friends* (1985), *A Misalliance* (1986), *A Friend from England* (1987), and *Latecomers* (1988).

A.S. Byatt

A.S. Byatt (née Drabble) was born in Sheffield on 24 August 1936. She was educated at The Mount School, York, and then read English at Newnham College, Cambridge. She did post-graduate work at Bryn Mawr College, Pennsylvania, where she was an English-Speaking Union fellow, and at Somerville College, Oxford. She was a lecturer and senior lecturer in English at London University until 1984, and has written literary criticism on various subjects, notably on Iris Murdoch. She married in 1959 I.C.R. Byatt, from whom she was later divorced, and in 1969 Peter J. Duffy. She is the mother of three daughters; a son died at the age of eleven. A.S. Byatt is a sister of Margaret Drabble. Her novels, all published by Chatto and Windus, are *Shadow of a Sun* (1964), *The Game* (1967), and the first two of a projected quartet: *The Virgin in the Garden* (1978) and *Still Life* (1985). Her short stories are published as *Sugar and other Stories* (Chatto and Windus, 1987).

Angela Carter

Angela Carter (née Stalker) was born in Eastbourne on 7 May 1940. She worked as a journalist in Croydon from 1958 to 1961, and then studied English at the University of Bristol. She has lived in Japan, and held posts as writer-in- residence at universities in England, the United States, and Australia. She writes reviews and journalism, and has also written children's books. She married Paul Carter in 1960, and was divorced in 1972. She has one son. Angela Carter's novels are *Shadow Dance* (1965), *The Magic Toyshop* (1967, awarded the John Llewellyn Rhys Memorial Prize), *Several Perceptions* (1968, winner of the Somerset Maugham Award), and *Heroes and Villains* (1969), all published by Heinemann, *Love* (1971), and *The Infernal Desire Machines of Dr Hoffmann* (1972), both published by Hart-Davis, *The Passion of New Eve* (Gollancz, 1977) and *Nights at the Circus* (Chatto and Windus, 1983). Her short stories are published as *Fireworks* (Quartet, 1974), *The Bloody Chamber* (Gollancz, 1979, winner of the

Cheltenham Royal Society of Literature Award), and *Black Venus* (Chatto and Windus, 1985).

Margaret Drabble

Margaret Drabble was born on 5 June 1939. She was educated at The Mount School, York, and read English at Newnham College, Cambridge. She married the actor Clive Swift in 1960, and for a time she acted with the Royal Shakespeare Company. She has written several works of literary criticism, a biography of Arnold Bennett, journalism and reviews, and she edited the revised fifth edition of *The Oxford Companion to English Literature* (1985). She has also written on political subjects, arguing the case for greater equality in society, e.g. in Fabian Society pamphlet no. 527 *Case for Equality*, 1988. She has three children. Her first marriage ended in divorce, and she married the biographer Michael Holroyd in 1982. Margaret Drabble is a sister of A.S. Byatt. Her novels, all published by Weidenfeld and Nicolson, are *A Summer Bird-Cage* (1963), *The Garrick Year* (1964), *The Millstone* (1965), *Jerusalem the Golden* (1967), *The Waterfall* (1969), *The Needle's Eye* (1972), *The Realms of Gold* (1975), *The Ice Age* (1977), *The Middle Ground* (1980), and *The Radiant Way* (1987).

Alice Thomas Ellis

Alice Thomas Ellis is the pseudonym of Anna Haycraft (née Lindholm), who was born in Liverpool in 1932. She went to Bangor Grammar School, and then studied at Liverpool School of Art. She married Colin Haycraft in 1957, and had seven children, of whom a daughter died in infancy, and a son at the age of nineteen. She is a director and the fiction editor of Duckworth publishers. She has written books on cookery, and she writes a regular column in *The Spectator*, under the title 'Home Life', and collected and published as *Home Life* (Fontana, 1987) and *More Home Life* (Fontana, 1988). She is also the author, with the psychiatrist Tom Pitt-Aikens, of *Secrets of Strangers* (Duckworth, 1986), a study of juvenile delinquency. Alice Thomas Ellis's novels, all published by Duckworth, are *The Sin Eater* (1977, winner of a Welsh Arts Council Award), *The Birds of the Air* (1980), *The 27th Kingdom* (1982), *The Other Side of the Fire* (1983),

Unexplained Laughter (1985), *The Clothes in the Wardrobe* (1987), and *The Skeleton in the Cupboard* (1988).

Zoe Fairbairns

Zoe Fairbairns was born in Tunbridge Wells on 20 December 1948. She was educated at St Catherine's School, Twickenham, and then studied at the College of William and Mary, Williamsburg, Virginia, and at the University of St Andrews, taking her degree in modern history. She was editor of *Sanity*, the newspaper of the Campaign for Nuclear Disarmament, from 1973 to 1975, and poetry editor of the feminist journal *Spare Rib* from 1978 to 1982. She has held several posts as writer-in-residence in schools and colleges. Zoe Fairbairns's novels are *Live as Family* (1968), and *Down: An Explanation* (1969), both published by Macmillan, *Benefits* (1979), and *Stand We at Last* (1983), both published by Virago, and *Here Today* (1984) and *Closing* (1987), both published by Methuen. With other members of the Feminist Writers' Group she is a contributor to the collection of short stories, *Tales I Tell My Mother* (Journeyman Press, 1978).

Sara Maitland

Sara Maitland was born in London in 1950, and was sent from her home in Scotland to school in Wiltshire, after which she read English at St Anne's College, Oxford. She is a reviewer, journalist, and biographer, and writes on theological subjects. She is married to an Anglican priest, and has two children. Sara Maitland's novels are *Daughter of Jerusalem* (Blond and Briggs, 1978) and *Virgin Territory* (Joseph, 1984). She has published two collections of stories, *Telling Tales* (Journeyman Press, 1983) and *A Book of Spells* (Methuen, 1987). With Michelene Wandor she wrote the epistolary fiction *Arky Types* (Methuen, 1987) and she is a contributor to the Feminist Writers' Group's collection of stories, *Tales I Tell My Mother* (Journeyman Press, 1978).

Emma Tennant

Emma Tennant was born on 20 October 1937. She spent her early childhood in the Scottish borders, and then went to St Paul's Girls' School in London. She studied privately at Oxford and in Paris. She worked in journalism, writing for *Queen* and *Vogue* in the 1960s, and she founded and edited the experimental literary magazine *Bananas* from 1975 to 1978. She has been general editor, since 1985, of Viking's series, *Lives of Modern Women*. She has three children. Emma Tennant published her first novel, *The Colour of Rain* (Weidenfeld and Nicolson, 1964) under the pseudonym Catherine Aydy. Her novels as Emma Tennant are (published by Cape except where otherwise indicated) *The Time of the Crack* (1973, re-issued as *The Crack* 1985), *The Last of the Country House Murders* (1974), *Hotel de Dream* (Gollancz, 1976), *Wild Nights* (1979), *Alice Fell* (1980), *Queen of Stones* (1982), *Women Beware Women* (1983), *Black Marina* (Faber, 1985), *The Adventures of Robina* (Faber, 1986), *The House of Hospitalities* (Viking, 1987), *A Wedding of Cousins* (Viking, 1988), *The Magic Drum* (Viking, 1989), and *Two Women of London* (Faber, 1989).

Fay Weldon

Fay Weldon (née Birkinshaw) was born in 1931 at Alvechurch, Worcestershire. She spent her childhood in New Zealand, and later attended Hampstead Girls' High School, London. She studied economics and psychology at St Andrews University, and worked for the Foreign Office, for the *Daily Mirror*, and in advertising. She has written numerous plays and adaptations for television. She has been married to Ron Weldon since 1960, and has four sons. Fay Weldon's novels (published by Hodder and Stoughton except where otherwise indicated) are *The Fat Woman's Joke* MacGibbon and Kee, 1967), *Down Among the Women* (Heinemann, 1971), *Female Friends* (Heinemann, 1975), *Remember Me* (1976), *Little Sisters* (1978), *Praxis* (1979), *Puffball* (1980), *The President's Child* (1982), *The Life and Loves of a She-Devil* (1983), *The Shrapnel Academy* (1986), *The Heart of the Country* (Hutchinson, 1987), *The Hearts and Lives of Men* (Heinemann, 1987), *The Rules of Life* (Hutchinson 1987), *Leader of the Band* (1988), and *The Cloning of Joanna May* (Collins 1989). She is also the author of two collections of short stories, *Watching Me Watching You* (1981), and *Polaris and other Stories* (1985).

Index

Index